The Irish Theatre Series 5

Edited by Robert Hogan, James Kilroy *and* Lia[...]

Denis Johnston's Irish Theatre

Denis Johnston's Irish Theatre

by Harold Ferrar

The Dolmen Press

TO

MIM AND JOHN

WITH LOVE AND VAST GRATITUDE

Set in Times Roman type, and printed and published in the Republic of
Ireland at The Dolmen Press, North Richmond Industrial Estate, North
Richmond Street, Dublin 1.

1973

Distributed outside Ireland, except in the United States of America and in
Canada by Oxford University Press. Distributed in the United States of
America and in Canada by Humanities Press Inc., 450 Park Avenue South,
New York, NY 10016.

SBN 85105 208 8

Contents

INTRODUCTION
    Main currents in the Irish drama of the
    nineteen twenties   *page* 7

PART ONE
    REBELS AND UNICORNS
    The Old Lady Says 'No!'   19
    The Moon in the Yellow River   40
    A Bride for the Unicorn   59
    The Sense of an Ending   78

PART TWO
    MORE REBELS AND THE BLIND GODDESS
    Storm Song and Blind Man's Buff   82
    The Golden Cuckoo   88
    The Dreaming Dust   97
    A Fourth for Bridge and
    Strange Occurrence on Ireland's Eye   107
    The Scythe and the Sunset   116

CHRONOLOGY   132

BRIEF STAGE HISTORIES   135

NOTES   137

A SELECTED BIBLIOGRAPHY   143

Acknowledgements

I would like to thank Daniel B. Dodson for his useful criticism, Chester Anderson for his warm encouragement, and Liam Miller for the generous expenditure of his bottomless expertise.

A number of people were unstinting of their time, insight and charm. Foremost is Denis Johnston, who allowed me to examine unpublished materials that lend this study what thoroughness it has. Hilton Edwards, Shelah Richards, Norah McGuinness, Lady Beatrice Gleneavy, Mrs. Lennox Robinson — lovely Dubliners all — were most helpful.

The Columbia University Council for Research in the Humanities awarded me a small grant which enabled me to do the final rewriting in Dublin.

To others who will understand more than mere thanks can convey: Brenna Katz Clarke for friendship and hard work, and Ian Alger for everything.

Above all I thank my infinitely talented editor — my wife — who will be as glad as I to see this book out of the typewriter and on the shelf.

Introduction

Main Currents in the Irish Drama of the Nineteen Twenties

When Denis Johnston was born on 18 June, 1901, the Irish theatre to which he was destined to make a major contribution was just two seasons and five plays old. Before Yeats established the Irish Literary Theatre in 1899 there had been no drama at all written about Ireland by Irishmen for an Irish audience. By the time Johnston made his inconspicuous acting debut on the Irish stage in February, 1925, the Irish drama had experienced a golden age, a rapid decline and a rebirth. In the first decade of the nineteen hundreds, the Irish theatre enjoyed a glorious (if misnamed) renaissance that put it permanently on the map of the theatrical world. After Synge's death in 1909, it hovered near its own artistic death in the throes of seemingly endless repetitions of peasant plays acted in what Oliver Gogarty called the 'begorrah' style. And then, in 1923, it was rudely shocked into new life by Seán O'Casey. O'Casey's impact on the moribund national theatre was electric; at last the Irish drama had a post-revolutionary, ironic, urban sensibility to keep pace with history. Johnston pays eloquent tribute to O'Casey's advent and the sense of new possibilities he opened to a disheartened national drama:

> Many of us still remember the thrill we got when *The Shadow of a Gunman* first took the stage. Here was the first play of a new post-war mentality — the first break away from a false set of values that had been slowly poisoning us — the first time we heard expressed on the stage emotions that we were as yet hardly conscious of feeling ourselves.[1]

For a theatre to take no risks is to regress, and the Abbey in the post-Synge years stood depressingly still. By the early twenties, prospects were dim for a vital, contemporary theatre in Ireland. The Abbey held undisputed reign with no challengers in sight, but she was a tired champion. The freshness and energy of the original impetus to create a national, truly people's theatre, had flagged. The poetic folk theatre of Yeats, Synge, Lady Gregory and the bevy of 'peasant' playwrights like Padraic Colum and William Boyle had been a theatre of high idealism, a magnificent cultural enterprise which tried to educate its audiences to an appreciation

7

of their native heritage, and to wean them from seven centuries of slave psychology into a proud new self-respect. Its story in the early years, often told, was a splendid one, for the Abbey will always live as a great activist theatre, one visionary's dream for a little while come true.

But when a nation loses the power to criticize itself, its drama deteriorates into propaganda, self-congratulation, or pap. Histories of the Irish drama invariably dwell on the *Playboy* riots of 1907 or the ruction over *The Plough and the Stars* in 1926 to exemplify the Abbey's courage. But all overlook the corollary: for twenty years the Abbey did not put on a play dangerous enough to provoke violent controversy. The theatre clung to 'plays about the life of artisans and country people'. The authentic dialogue of Colum became, by the late teens, stage-Irish, unintentional self-parody. Conflicts once immediately pertinent hardened into melodramatic formulae until the Abbey's boards groaned with the machinations of gombeen men, ungrateful sons leaving the farm, and the shady doings of the local politician or land-grabber. Perhaps the Abbey was a perfect reflection of national self-blindness, or maybe it was only missing the gifted playwright who combined patriotism with a keen eye for the nation's failings. Whichever, while it was waiting for O'Casey the Abbey had become a conservative, insular theatre.

This isolationism (though understandable given the political exigencies of a national theatre in a country fighting for its freedom) was particularly exacerbated during a period of wonderful flowering in world theatre when dramatists like Pirandello, Brecht, O'Neill and Giraudoux were burgeoning elsewhere. The threat of an hermetic Irish culture feeding on itself until it was devoured had been recognized long before the process began to claim its victims. In the early days of the Abbey, Joyce (in 'The Day of the Rabblement') and Æ had pleaded for an international outlook. In Æ's words: 'We cannot be intellectually self-sustaining any more than England, France, Italy or Germany could. . . . We must penetrate the Irish culture with world wisdom, or it will cease to be a culture, and our literature will lose its vitality and become a literature of conventions.' [2]

Yeats had always intended to produce continental plays, but the Ibsen vogue, rampant throughout Europe at the turn of the century, repelled him. In his determination to mould a theatre that would be at once Irish and spiritual, Yeats carefully shunned the New Realism in favour of an heroic, mythic and lyrical drama, unmistakeably stamped with his own aesthetic inclinations. Yeats never understood Ibsen's way of paying homage to the human spirit; and it is a sad irony that the offerings of the Abbey were all too soon to fall into their own spiritless brand of realism. At any rate, an urgent campaign for native plays proved so successful that for twenty years the Abbey was able to subsist almost entirely on contemporary Irish plays written for it. The plan to put on non-Irish plays was virtually forgotten, with the exception of an occasional foray into Molière and Goldoni (in Lady Gregory's Galway dialect adaptations) or a flirtation with Maeterlinck, a symbolistic favourite of Yeats's. In 1913 there was a brief flurry of foreign productions (one Hauptmann and two Strindbergs) but this quickly petered out and made no lasting impact, though it was an encouraging sign of Yeats's non-parochial horizons. Not until 1921 did another European play reach the Abbey stage.

After World War I, however, the Abbey management finally listened to the clamouring of its young actors and writers for exposure to the impressive variety of recent continental drama. The national theatre supported an experiment that was to have pervasive influence on the works of O'Casey, Lennox Robinson and Denis Johnston. In October, 1918, Robinson, with the full co-operation of Yeats, formed the Dublin Drama League, 'for the purpose of seeing plays which we otherwise would have no chance of seeing'. Defending his project at a public forum to solicit subscriptions, Robinson said:

> Here in Ireland we are isolated, cut off from the thought of the world, except the English world, and from England we get little in drama, except fourth-rate. I ask you, for the young writer's sake, to open up the door and let us out of our prison. Seeing foreign plays will not divorce our minds from Ireland.[3]

The Abbey, under the constant surveillance of a vociferous, nationalistic, bourgeois audience, could make no commitment of its own to a project devoted to non-Irish work, and *avant-garde* to boot. But it did what it could. It made available its stage and company to the part-time Drama League, which performed on Sunday and Monday nights, when the Abbey was dark. In addition to the immeasurable boon of broadening and deepening the resources of the Abbey actors, the League eventually paid direct dividends; three of its productions had regular runs at the Abbey.

The Drama League was an imaginative solution to the cultural lag in the Irish theatre. The plan permitted the Abbey to continue its dedication to 'a Celtic and Irish school of dramatic literature' while providing a valuable and heartily welcomed training ground in modern techniques for Dublin's young theatre people. It performed the experimental works of Andreyev, Lenormand, Benavente, Strindberg, O'Neill and Pirandello, and mounted two new plays of Yeats, *The Cat and the Moon* and *The Only Jealousy of Emer*. (The Abbey itself put on no new play by Yeats, with the exception of his adaptations from Sophocles, from December, 1919, until August, 1929.) As actor and producer for the League and for the New Players (a later offshoot of the League), Denis Johnston mastered the expressionism of Kaiser and Toller. He pays the League generous tribute:

> Lennox and the Drama League really did remarkable work in the twenties and early thirties in introducing to Dublin all the avant-garde plays of the time. He did not understand or like expressionism. He left this to Arthur Shields and later to me. But he . . . taught us and showed us Strindberg, Pirandello, Benavente, Schnitzler — people whose plays we would never have seen — and maybe not even have read, if it hadn't been for the Drama League.[4]

This affectionate assessment is not unique. One gets from Johnston, Shelah Richards (who acted frequently in the League) and from Mrs. Lennox Robinson (Dorothy Travers-Smith, who designed for it) the unmistakeable sense that the League was the real life of the Dublin drama world for most of the twenties. Theatre people reminisce with gusto about the choices of the League's productions and they recall with humour the haste and haphazardness of some of the results. The national theatre had become a stately mansion and the League a home for natural exuberance and curiosity, a haven which provided the inestimably valuable freedom to make mistakes. And as a kind of safety valve, the Drama League offered actors a variety and excitement which allowed them to return to their Abbey duties refreshed and vigorous. In addition, the League prepared Dublin for the Gate Theatre, a full-time professional company — Ireland's first 'international theatre' — whose star playwright was to be Denis Johnston.

The Irish theatre then, entered the twenties on a note of renewal despite the stolid official position of the Abbey. While Robinson provided most of the energy needed to get the League going, it is clear that without Yeats's firm backing and substantial involvement (he was president of the League during its first eight years) the enterprise would not have been possible. While Yeats made some abominable decisions at the Abbey (for instance, his neglect of Fitzmaurice's plays), had he had final say the national theatre would have moved in a more experimental direction. But the dominant personality of Lady Gregory, who was ever conscious of the theatre's original purpose, kept the primary 'Irish' aim to the fore. Yeats was always receptive to the unusual, the modern, the difficult; what he despised in any art form was the undisciplined or the lifeless. Every Drama League play selection required his presidential approval. Thus, as the list of the League's productions during his tenure proves, he was not even opposed to the angular discontinuities and programmatic urgency of the German expressionists whose work was so different from his own, for in them he discerned spiritual value, a rejection of Mammon.

The influence of Yeats in the expansion of the horizons of the Irish theatre during the twenties cannot be overestimated. As he watched the very naturalism he despised entrench itself as the celebrated Abbey style, Yeats in his own plays began to move toward exaggerated stylization and intensified symbolic gesture. Around 1915, a few years before the formation of the Drama League, Yeats abandoned Irish folk material and began to develop his dance plays under the influence of his study of the Japanese Noh drama. From this time on he was in the peculiar position of running a theatre which could not do his plays. It is possible to consider Yeats the most adventurous experimental playwright in Dublin in the twenties. World theatre (and especially the films) rapidly absorbed the techniques of expressionism and made them part of the standard vocabulary of stagecraft, whereas the achievement of Yeats, his amazing combinations of ritual, movement, song, mask and rhythm — tremendous demands on the craft of the actor — are just beginning to be understood in their implications for theatre practice.

As a matter of record, what few tremors of experiment that did

11

quiver the Abbey in the mid-twenties — not to be sure powerfully enough to cleave the surface in any permanent way — were the accomplishment of Yeats, with the backing of his protegé, the internationally-minded Robinson. In January, 1927, the Abbey took over a League production of O'Neill's expressionistic *The Emperor Jones,* the first true invasion of the modern into the national theatre. The following year the Abbey did a *King Lear* with futuristic designs by Travers-Smith, and in 1929 the theatre capped this short-lived but significant surge of modernism with a balletic version of Yeats's *Fighting the Waves,* danced by Ninette de Valois to an ultra-contemporary score by George Antheil.*

It was the Abbey's production of *King Lear* in November, 1928, its first venture into Shakespeare, which brought Denis Johnston to the public eye. Johnston was well-known to the more intellectual Dublin theatregoers, regulars of the Drama League, but he was unknown to the Abbey audience until he was chosen to direct *Lear.* The circumstances surrounding the selection of Johnston provide an interesting revelation of the behind closed doors functioning of the Abbey directorate, and an exposure of the company's internal stresses and power manipulations. The new climate of experiment fostered by Yeats and the League had encouraged Johnston (then a young barrister) to write a long one-act expressionistic satire, *Shadowdance,* which he submitted to the Abbey in 1926. Yeats was the reader; his comments show he found the script too obvious and rough in structure. Johnston revised the play several times, calling the version he re-submitted *Symphony in Green.* The Abbey company after its Drama League training was perfectly capable of mounting the play, and Yeats and Robinson were sympathetic, but not stubbornly enough to counter Lady Gregory's swift refusal. Yeats was impressed enough with Johnston to feel that the Abbey owed him something in return for rejecting the play. He also wanted to continue the thrust of experiment begun the previous season with *The Emperor Jones.* Convinced that Johnston could be counted upon to devise an up-to-date production, Yeats (with Robinson's concurrence) entrusted *Lear* to him, to the chagrin of Lady Gregory and some

---

* 'Such strange materials . . . this riot of discords' commented the diarist Joseph Holloway, who could invariably be counted upon to malcomprehend the new.

12

members of the company, notably Arthur 'Boss' Shields, who directed frequently for the Drama League and resented being passed over. A bureaucratic sense of hierarchy, of service and reward, had formed imperceptibly over the years and had become an important factor in the theatre's operation, and could make the going treacherous for a newcomer who lacked unanimous support. Johnston was aware that Yeats wanted an extension of the more daring modes beginning to surface at the Abbey, but he was unaware that he was chosen partially to ease Yeats's regret over the rejected play. Lady Gregory, according to Joseph Holloway's report, was 'all against [Johnston] as a Producer at the Abbey and openly says so.'[5] Indeed she was, her *Journals* tell the tale:

> Oct. 29, 1928.
> I met with a group of the players. They are . . . not happy over *King Lear*. I had never even been told it was being put on by Lennox Robinson and Yeats. Arthur Shields is indignant because the production has been given to Denis Johnston, who has no connection with us, and I fancy it was given to him to make up for the rejection of his Emmet play. Dolan [Michael 'Mick' Dolan, who led the company's resistance to *The Plough and the Stars* two years earlier] is furious because his part, the Fool, is being cut to almost nothing. Starkie [Walter Starkie, an Abbey director] and I agree that we must assert ourselves in future and not let business be settled over our heads.

Despite her annoyance, she had the integrity to enter her true reaction to the opening:

> Nov. 27.
> *Lear* last night wonderful, McCormick magnificent — there is no other word — all through. The play that I had thought would be too long seemed short . . . the others, Michael Dolan and Barry Fitzgerald were fine. And the staging . . . I slept but little and seized the papers this morning — the *Irish Times* cool but kind, the *Independent* belittling with cold criticism.[6]

Six weeks before *King Lear* opened, there occurred the most important event in the Dublin theatre of the late twenties, the launching of the Dublin Gate Theatre. The Gate was the heir to

the international outlook of the Drama League, which slowly
phased itself out as its function became superfluous, for Dublin
didn't need both a professional and amateur 'little' theatre. The
Drama League (and the New Players) had laid the groundwork
for the Gate. Whereas the Abbey put on native plays for an
increasingly middle-class audience, the League had appealed to a
small, educated, cosmopolitan group, supporters of the *avant-garde*.
The Gate, which has never made money, might not have lasted
at all had the League not been going for a decade. In the two
seasons preceding the opening of the Gate, the League put on
The Emperor Jones, He Who Gets Slapped and *Hoppla!* (among
others). Among the productions of its first two seasons, the Gate
presented *The Hairy Ape, The Adding Machine* and *R.U.R.*
Except for the central difference that the Gate was a full-time
professional theatre, in terms of their dramatic emphases the two
groups formed a continuum. World drama had come to Dublin
to stay. Thus, in the winter of 1928, despite the tragic loss of
O'Casey over *The Silver Tassie* fracas, the Dublin theatre was
more lively than it had been for twenty years: the Abbey was
doing Ibsen and a controversial Shakespeare; the Drama League
had vastly broadened the scope of the Irish stage; and the Gate
was on its way with a brilliant *Peer Gynt* on the miniscule stage of
the 102 seat Peacock theatre. Holloway, attending the Gate's first
night, said, 'All present wished the Gate well.' One Dublin wit,
however, sensitive to the deep-seated philistinism of Dublin play-
goers, quipped: 'Sure, and what are the odd hundred seats for?'

The Gate's history has been well-told in numerous articles and
in the autobiographies of its founders, Hilton Edwards and Micheál
MacLiammoir. They met as young actors touring Ireland and soon
discovered they shared a mutual dissatisfaction with the state of
Irish drama. In their view, Irish naturalism, in subject matter and
staging, had reached a dead end. A new professional theatre was
needed to specialize in a stylized urban drama. They formed the
Gate (modelled on Peter Godfrey's London Gate Theatre) not to
rival but to complement the Abbey. They hoped, by producing the
best of modern classics and the latest departures from realism,
to develop a varied group of Irish dramatists liberated from the
Abbey formula, 'limited only by the limits of the imagination.' [7]
These were purposes which dovetailed perfectly with the direction
Denis Johnston had taken in the play the Abbey had refused. Had

it been written to order, *The Old Lady Says 'No!'* (as the final version was titled)* could not have been a more perfect realisation of the Gate's design. Today, this first Irish expressionist play seems the natural fruition toward which all the innovation of the twenties had been ripening. Like the best work of Synge and O'Casey, *The Old Lady Says 'No!'* was a profound critique of Irish life. All three writers love Ireland deeply, but as it is, not with all unpleasantness glossed over. In addition, the play continues the raucous metropolitan background first introduced by O'Casey. The combination of these three strains (the Irish content, the urban environment and the radical stagecraft) and the timing of the play's appearance make *The Old Lady Says 'No!'* a landmark in the story of the Irish theatre — at once a summing up of the advances of the decade and a herald of future possibilities. With a new theatre, a playwright who had written 'an astonishingly brilliant play . . . [which] must certainly be one of the best first plays ever written,'[8] and signs of flexibility in the Abbey, the Irish theatre, despite the departure of O'Casey, stood at a critical point, a zenith of anticipation.

*   *   *

Of the numerous attempts to grasp as a whole the course of Irish drama, none has taken into sufficient account the complicated currents of the last half of the twenties. There is no study of the Drama League's contribution, no treatment of staging and design during the little flurry of anti-realism at the Abbey. Only the early seasons of the Gate have been given their due. Historians of the Irish theatre tend to focus exclusively on literary value, political backgrounds, personalities or theme, at the expense of the intricate matter of staging. The standard chroniclers of the Abbey (like A. E. Malone) usually trace the linear development of the Abbey from the turn of the century years of poetic folk drama to the endless dominion of the realistic peasant play, with O'Casey placed squarely in the line of Abbey realism as extender of

*Lady Gregory was affectionately called 'the old lady' behind her back, and the title of this play derives from a report of her opinion at a meeting to consider the possible production of the play at the Abbey. The title has since gone into the local language as a figure of speech meaning: it won't do in Ireland, with a suggestion of prejudice and narrowmindedness.

15

pastoral naturalism to the city. A subtler analyst, John Gassner, sees an acute division into a 'first galaxy' through 1923 and a 'second coming' after the formation of the Free State; O'Casey of course leads the resurrection. This second period comprises a post-revolutionary theatre of reaction: to ideals that cloyed or had failed and to played out techniques. At its mildest a theatre of disenchantment or malaise, at its most powerful and memorable it was a theatre of vitriolic disillusion, of outrage at dead hope embalmed in mock-heroic dreams. What characterizes most studies of the Irish drama is a zealous search for continuity, even in patterns of action and reaction. The compression of so fecund a body of drama into little more than a generation explains the quest for principles of unity and inter-relationship. Dame Una Ellis-Fermor is the most convincing advocate for the position that:

> The Irish drama has been a continuous movement, showing continuous development from its beginnings in 1899 to the present day, and even the most recent drama cannot be sharply detached from that continuum. . . . Irish drama forms . . . a web, that, though of varying colours, is seamless.[9]

Using the same periodic distinction as Gassner, Dame Una seeks to locate some unity of evolution. She considers the Irish theatre of the thirties to be 'partly poetic, partly satiric, analytic or even iconoclastic in relation to the original movement. That is to say, it has been a vital and progressive growth. . . . Both [phases] . . . combine . . . to make a whole which is indivisible, a living and representative body of national drama.'[10] Though her 'even iconoclastic' seems understatement, her focus on the national image as the common concern of all Irish dramatists pinpoints the most fruitful area for comparison and contrast. For instance, although the thematic links are clear between two Catholic plays like *Maurice Harte* (1912) and *Shadow and Substance* (1932), it is only as 'readings of Irish life' that *Maurice Harte* and *The Old Lady Says 'No!'* have any similarity. With the exception of occasional departures into a personal mythology, like Yeats's *Unicorn for the Stars* and *Purgatory,* or Johnston's *A Bride for the Unicorn,* the Irish drama is characterized by its fierce commitment to showing Ireland to herself, by its relentless absorption in what Lennox Robinson called 'the Irish thing'.

'We must criticize ourselves ruthlessly,'[11] Robinson demanded,

16

and this admonition is the perfect epigraph to the story of the Irish drama after 1922. Irish dramatists were not only fed up with the unkept promises of the early years of the century, they were also in reaction against the atrophy of the stage as a formal medium. What is universally overlooked is that the revolt of the Irish playwright against the severe limits of his craft began not with O'Casey but with Yeats's break from the original ideals of the dramatic renaissance and his venture into the dance plays. While the accounts of the historians are often sophisticated, they might well be supported by the detailed consideration of Yeats's technical contribution which had little direct or lasting effect on the Abbey itself but inaugurated a climate of experiment that eventually permitted Edwards and MacLiammoir to hazard a permanent alternative to the Abbey.

Thus, it was on the double note of the reassessment of national identity and the rejuvenating influx of new forms that Denis Johnston first offered his mordant images of morbid Ireland in *The Old Lady Says 'No!'* In method, it was the most original native play Dublin had yet seen; in content it ruthlessly exposed Ireland's legions of shortcomings. *The Countess Cathleen* and *The Playboy of the Western World* had illustrated the problems of undertaking a critical analysis of Ireland in the theatre. W. G. Fay said in his memoirs that any play put before the public 'had to face two questions: Was it an insult to the faith? Was it a slander on the people of Ireland?' [12] The situation, according to Johnston, was identical in 1929:

> You were dealing with an audience that was very sensitive about the image of Ireland that was being built up after liberty had come. The Irish audience was vigilant not to allow the Catholic Celtic tradition to be what they considered let down. [13]

It was to this audience Johnston brought *The Old Lady Says 'No!'*, insulting and slanderous. In setting out 'to paint Ireland and her problems in their true colours', [14] Johnston was one of the few courageous writers who fulfilled Lady Gregory's noble aspirations for an Irish theatre:

> I had had from the beginning a vision of historical plays being sent to us through all the counties of Ireland. For to

17

have a real success and come into the life of the country, one must touch a real and eternal emotion, and history comes only next to religion in our country.[15]

1 : Rebels and Unicorns

THE OLD LADY SAYS 'NO!'

The Old Lady Says 'No!' was the final production of the Gate's second season; at its première it immediately established itself as part of the living repertory of the Irish theatre. Like O'Casey's three Dublin war plays, *The Old Lady* captures a progressively intensifying mood of disappointment as the ideals of seven heroic centuries prove as unworkable as they are indestructible. 'Cinderella', Johnston said, 'has turned into the Free State.' [1] In this play he sharply juxtaposes the dismal reality of the Irish situation in the twenties — revolt, civil war, assassination, atrocities — against the rage for sentiment — religious, political, cultural, emotional — which is precisely the source of self-perpetuating violence. Johnston shows Ireland as a child who wants her own way but doesn't know *what* she wants. The play is iconoclastic, deeply felt, wildly funny, lyrical, contemporary — an impassioned offering to Dublin by a bruised lover.

As might have been expected, the vociferous nationalist element reacted in character, precisely as it had when Yeats, Synge and O'Casey had tried to tell the truth. Riots were threatened, thereby proving the play had touched an exposed nerve of the body politic. Thirty years after the Irish theatre was launched, it was still waiting for that 'uncorrupted and imaginative' audience Lady Gregory dreamed of.

In an unpublished piece apparently intended as an introduction to the play, Johnston recalls the excitement of rehearsal days: 'I was warned by various friends that the play would be denounced as anti-national, or as Republican propaganda, or as a personal reflection of so-and-so. . . .' There was no riot or loud denounciation from the audience, no need for anyone (as Yeats had twice had to do at the Abbey) to tell the Dublin audience it had disgraced itself. In spite of the fact that *The Old Lady* handles rather roughly most of Ireland's sacred cows, from Robert Emmet to Cathleen ni Houlihan herself, what protests there were complained more of the allegedly blasphemous parody of Holy Writ than of anti-Irishism. These protests came in the forms of 'strong representations to the authorities', vitriolic letters to the editor, and 'indignant women [walking] out during the last act'. One such outburst is worth quoting; it is a classic expression of those two fixed ideas, country and church, right or wrong, that modern Irish writers have had to fight every step of their way. Constantine Curran, friend of Joyce and drama critic for *The Irish Statesman*, had given *The Old Lady* a very favourable notice. This pained one James P. O'Reilly, a contributor to the paper, and Mr. O'Reilly wrote to the editor:

> I am amazed . . . that such a play . . . was not condemned. . . . It is a play that could not be produced in any theatre open to the public outside this country. The symbolic figure of Ireland is represented by . . . "a foul-mouthed harridan". Imagine Britannia represented on the London stage as a lecherous, dirty tongued old drab. . . . This, however, is a minor matter in comparison with another. Here in the capital city of this Christian country, while the hymns of the multitudes who gathered so splendidly to worship God seem still fading in the wind, a coterie of persons, directed I understand, by a foreigner, have seen fit to insult the theatre-going public, with a blasphemous outrage. A crazy "Robert Emmet" raves and rants on the stage the most sacred passages of Holy Writ, preceded and followed by shouts and ejaculations from the other members of the cast of "bloody" and "bastard" and the like. . . . My opinion . . . certainly will be scoffed at by those who think their own standards of literary or artistic merit are above and outside the law of God and the law of the land . . . but I give it here so that it may not be said that professing Christians who contribute to this paper are cowed or silenced on such occasions when protest is a matter of conscience and good citizenship.[2]

There are always more than a fair share of O'Reillys in a Dublin audience; if they had their blind way Irish drama would be as dead as Boucicault. Holloway, who hailed the Gate a year before, was soon to be carping about 'the taste of [its] dung-minded, well-dressed patrons'. But there were those too who cherished honesty and fearlessness. The Gate audience was witnessing the debut of a young playwright with a subtle intelligence and supple dramatic technique who commanded a serious hearing, and some of them recognized it. As P. J. O'Hegarty wrote, 'If Mr. Johnston was an

Englishman and had written this play on English life, he would be famous on five continents, instead of being sniffed at on an island.' [3]

The Old Lady is a swift-paced, multiscenic expressionistic satire, deeply indebted to plays like Kaufman and Connelly's *Beggar on Horseback* (itself owing much to the movies) and to *The Land of Many Names*, a little-known work by Josef Capek, as well as to the pioneering achievements of Kaiser and Toller, and *The Dream Play* of Strindberg. A playwright whose theme is the death grip that cliché holds on national life, not least on Irish art, naturally would repudiate the hackneyed local realistic play in favour of an ultramodern European form. The play's producer, Hilton Edwards, so effectively blended the prose, poetry, music, dance and spectacle that the result is still vividly remembered by people who attended the first night. The play has great motion and variety in the progression of its scenes. Edwards, with MacLiammoir, the Gate's designer and romantic lead, lost none of the many opportunities for abrupt, ironic contrast in the confrontation of Emmet with the Dublin of the mid-twenties. Visually there are the broad shifts in set from garden to familiar Dublin streets to salon to slum and back to Curran's garden at the close. At any given moment there is a disparity between the colourful green jacket, plumed hat and sword of the hero and the drab blazers, caps, rags or finery of the Dubliners he meets. Verbally there is a clash of styles and dialects: prose and poetry; the clichés of the plain and fancy city dwellers and the Irish rhythms of Synge; lines from Irish writers, the Bible, world literature. There are similar shifts in lighting, beginning in shadow and going through broad daylight, night, the artificial light of the salon, the candle-lit tenement and back to shadow again. A vital and exciting stage picture is created by the swiftness of these multiple changes accompanied by street noises, a crescendo drumbeat and piano renditions of national songs.

MacLiammoir describes Edwards's energetic direction of *The Old Lady*:

It gave the chance of a lifetime to Hilton . . . a producer who can handle choral speaking, rhythmical movement, metrical climax and a magnificence of a massed effect with the precision of a ballet-master. . . . Hilton had discovered a seemingly unconscious rhythm in the lines spoken by the shadows and had introduced them with a pulsation of light and the notes

21

of a drum beaten with varying *tempi*. . . . The effect he achieved in performance was overwhelmingly exciting.[4]

Edwards is specific about the 'effect' he was aiming for: 'I tried to give the play the quality of the delirium of being under anaesthesia.'[5] Highest praise for the staging comes from Johnston himself, who as a rule is extremely critical of the productions of his plays: '. . . the pattern devised by Hilton Edwards and Michael MacLiammoir for its first production in 1929 has become as much an integral part of the play as is the text, and is not likely to be bettered.'[6]

*   *   *

History ironically reveals the Abbey's rejection of *The Old Lady* as Johnston's luckiest misfortune. It might have been given a lackadaisical production by the Abbey, 'played with that subtle air of distaste with which experienced actors can dissociate themselves from the sentiments expressed in their parts,'[7] and been promptly forgotten. Instead it was given an ideal production at the Gate. By the time *The Old Lady* reached the public, it had undergone an involved series of changes, difficult to trace accurately, from the original *Shadowdance* through *Symphony in Green* (the rejected version) to the final Gate play. There are three extant versions of the play; the first is the unpublished 1926 manuscript of *Shadowdance*, full of typed and inked revisions. Johnston revised the play extensively before its production in 'two parts with choral interludes', then made further changes during rehearsal and production, as he does with all his plays, for he believes that

> all plays require rewriting after their first presentation for the obvious reason that they do not really exist until they have had to face up to the reactions of a sensible objective audience. . . . All these [changes] indicate a healthy state of affairs — that the play is a living thing, undergoing modifications that all serious drama must undergo in the course of production, and that the author is fussy about his canon.[8]

The processes of change in production are beyond reconstruction, but are incorporated in the first published edition of 1932. The final version appears in the 1959 volume of collected plays; it differs from the 1932 version only in the updating of numerous topical references. Most of the 'blasphemous outrages' have been removed too, perhaps in good-humoured compliance to a 1935 letter from the Lord Chamberlain's office in reference to a London production: 'There are seven bloodies in the play and at least half of these should be omitted.' In an interview, Johnston told me that he was 'through fiddling with the play', so the '59 version may be considered final.

The skeleton structure of the play is left relatively unchanged throughout the expansion of *Shadowdance* into *The Old Lady Says 'No!'* The basic order of the movement of the action remains intact in all versions: the opening playlet, the accidental blow on the head, the dream sequence. However, a detailed collation of *Shadowdance* and the '32 version of *The Old Lady* reveals a surer sense of theme and a remarkable advance in craftsmanship, reflected in the increasing accuracy and control of methods aimed at evoking specific responses. The growth of the satirical idea of the play, for instance, is clearly evidenced in the changes between the '29 and '32 versions. *The Old Lady* is Johnston's reaction to the political and social conditions of the '20's in the form of a satire of national immaturity, particularly of that dominant characteristic of the Irish mind, nationalist fervour, that keeps Ireland parochial and insulated. For his target Johnston found a sustained dramatic metaphor in the romantic, sentimental patriotism of the nineteenth century Irish poets and melodramatists. 'The opening playlet is made up almost entirely of thematic lines' from these poets (most of the originals can be found in *The Dublin Book of Verse,* a popular anthology published in the heyday of the Irish renaissance, 1909). Johnston made numerous changes in this structurally and thematically crucial playet. In the evolution from *Shadowdance* into *The Old Lady,* the selections from the nineteenth century are more than quadrupled from ten to forty-five. Since many of these allusions recur and function thematically, Johnston vastly increased the complexity and richness of the play's design and texture. For example, Sarah Curran's opening speech in *Shadowdance* was a mournful outcry for the return of her lost lover ('My wild lover, return to me'). In *The Old Lady* her speech is composed of four lines from Mangan's 'The Fair Hills of Eire, Oh!' (which become a leitmotif for Sarah) and three lines from Darley's 'Serenade of a Loyal Martyr'. The substitution of

Mangan's poem is most pertinent to *The Old Lady,* for the poem is 'a lament . . . for Eire's decay . . . in bitterness outpoured'. In a similar change, Johnston added a phrase from Lady Wilde's 'The Exodus': 'A million a decade.' The Speaker (Emmet) in *The Old Lady* uses the phrase in reference to the British army's occupation of Ireland, but Lady Wilde's poem is about the population loss of Ireland, 'a nation fading away from history's page . . . a nation dying of inner decay'. The Wilde quotation serves a double purpose: in context it satirizes one of Ireland's 'rancid political clichés' and for the literate in the audience, who know its source, it incorporates a central theme of the play. Johnston perfected this method of significant allusion in the '32 version of *The Old Lady*; it appears in *Shadowdance,* but not as a major principle of structural organization.

Every quotation is carefully selected to play upon emotion-charged associations. Johnston explains the rationale of the play's composition and the goals of the allusive technique:

> The real play must be regarded as what goes on in the mind of the audience . . . the clash of idea on idea, of emotion on emotion in the listener's intelligence constitutes the action. And these ideas and emotions can be stimulated without a narrative plot . . . melodically as in music or by simple association of ideas.
>
> In *The Old Lady Says 'No!'* I have attempted to evolve a thematic method based on association of ideas . . . it presupposes a set of recognisable figments in the minds of the audience . . . a motif in the realm of thought is carried best by a name or quotation.[9]
>
> We wanted to know whether the emotional appeal of music could be made use of in terms of theatrical prose, and an opera constructed that did not have to be sung. Could the associations and thought patterns already connected with the song and slogans of our city be used deliberately to evoke a planned reaction from a known audience?[10]

The clarification in Johnston's mind of a thematic-allusive method for embodying his critical vision of contemporary Ireland accounts for the new complexity of allusion in the '32 version of *The Old Lady*. The confidence instilled by his more precise idea of theme and method enabled Johnston not only to expand the germ of the allusive technique, but also to curb the rhetorical flights and heavy-handed satire of *Shadowdance*.

Before Johnston fully conceived *The Old Lady* as a satire on melodramatic sentiment and political idealism, a portion of the original version was a funny but pointless satire of the plethoric dialogue and heroics of numerous Victorian plays about Emmet. In *Shadowdance*, the British Major Sirr, villain of many an Emmet melodrama, captures and taunts Emmet in Curran's garden:

> Sirr.   What fools! . . . Why this one hadn't even the sense to keep to the hills. . . . All we have to do is to put a watch upon his Mistress and . . . he walks into the trap.
> Speaker. Take back that word! Take back that word!
> Sirr.   A pretty wench, too. Not that she'll be lonely long.

Yeats had criticized this entire opening scene: 'When I first read this scene I thought the ornate writing was a deliberate caricature, a parody of . . . popular romance. It should be cut out everywhere except some few sentences necessary to plot.' [11] Although Yeats's stress on plot was an obvious misreading of the play, his distaste for Johnston's 'youthful extravagance' was instrumental in leading the playwright to his thematic technique which demands the excision of non-functional, self-indulgent dialogue.

There is a final noteworthy alteration from *Shadowdance*, a change in the ending. The original version was rife with ludicrous alliteration and overstatement that dominated the mediocre attempt at satire of Irish oratory. Its elimination is an excellent gauge of Johnston's improved craftsmanship and his shift from direct statement to subtle and carefully paced evocation. In the original, Emmet justifies his actions to the accusing shadows:

> I stand here as Robert Emmet, posturing upon the stage, playing my precious part before you all in this little Hell of babbling torment. . . . You think that I am mad, but O, my friends, think well before you fling that berserk boomerang about this giddy globe.
> You think that I am a fool . . . that dared batter on the bars of incommutable reality . . . but, O, my friends, let mercy mingle with your merriment, for what one of us can

25

tell when he derides the feeble folly of a poor romanticist that he is not flogging the carcase of his own dead heart?

Might I, like you, run to take refuge with the cowards and the weary of heart, and those of little faith in that sanctuary for broken dreamers which the world calls cynicism.

Yeats, after caustically noting that ' "cynicism" was a worn out commonplace thirty years ago,' justly dismissed this passage with the single word, 'rubbish'. Johnston rewrote the ending, discarding rhetoric in favour of lyricism, replacing obviousness with ironical suggestion: he conquered his excesses, and substituted thematically functional dialogue for this and other 'rubbish'.

Johnston's improved version is organized upon two main structural principles: Emmet's dream journey, which may roughly be called the plot; and the use of controlled allusion to evoke in the audience's mind planned associations. The dream journey creates the framework of fantasy that permits departure from realistic cause and effect and allows a musical or thematic principle of organization. The journey comprises the forward motion of the play and is the occasion for broad satirical contrasts. But the subtler satirical purpose, the explosion of racial myths and cliché, is effected by a sustained organization of a vast range of references. A cross-section at any point in the forward action of the dream journey reveals a network of allusions and quotations which operate satirically.

Apropos of the mass of allusions to Dublin life, Hilton Edwards once remarked that 'The Old Lady reads like a railway guide'.[12] He might have added that it also reads like a florilegium of pearls from the Irish writers, poets, playwrights and orators; legion too are references and allusions to Irish myth, folklore, politics, religion and history as well as quotations from an odd assortment of sources including the Bible, Dante, Shaw, Blake, Henry Wadsworth Longfellow, A. A. Milne and 'the songs and slogans' of Ireland. Much of the dialogue is made up of these allusions; a speech without at least one is the exception and each allusion has a thematic point usually dependent upon the premise that the audience is Dublin Irish. The British critic W. A. Darlington opened his review of the 1935 London production of The Old Lady with the observation that 'this must, I should think, be the most Irish play ever written'. Johnston notes that 'the play to be

26

intelligible to a non-Irish audience requires to some extent to be translated.' The charge of obscurity is the one most frequently leveled against the play, but to criticize its 'too intimate localism' is to ask *The Old Lady* to be a different play with a different purpose.

It is possible to take virtually any reference from the play and indicate the way it contributes to characterization and at the same time both presents an attitude firmly held by Irishmen and satirizes this attitude, often hilariously. One such instance has been touched upon briefly, the quotation from Lady Wilde's 'Exodus': 'a million a decade.' In context, as Emmet's challenge to the British forces, 'Let them come. A million a decade', it characterizes Emmet's impulsive heroism yet reduces it to absurdity by the sheer magnitude of the number. Having served its purpose of deflating the braggart hero, the allusion is next aimed satirically at the Irish hero worshippers without whom there would be no Irish heroes. The subject of the British military presence in Ireland is even today a great favourite of Dublin's public house orators; its mention will touch off a barrage of clichés encompassing the whole course of Irish subjugation. Johnston's deeper target is the lovable boon companion Irishman, representative of the irresponsibly inert nationalism that revels endlessly in the dubious glories of the past, of which Emmet is the chief symbol. As Johnston, spoofing O'Casey's style, has O'Cooney say in the salon scene, 'Ah, not for all the wealth of the world would I give up the maddenin' minglin' memories of the past.' Ireland's real-life bar-room rebels linger in glamourized distortions of the past, in the imaginary grievances of the present or the unlikely glories of the future, while Ireland, something like a nation at last, has the most important task of her history at hand — the solidification of her nationhood. This is the point that is reached by the series of planned associations which dictate the selection of the line. The allusion, then, functions in four ways: to characterize Emmet; to satirize this characterization (the popular view of Emmet), thereby deflating Irish reverence of this hero; to evoke a familiar association in the audience, usually involving a cliché of Irish life; to satirize this cliché and the attitude that keeps it alive; that is, to criticize the romantic Irish racial myth and its irrelevance to the realities of present day Irish life.

A little later in the play there is another prime example of the complex functioning of the allusive technique. The 'old tattered Flower Woman', a familiar figure in the everyday street life of Dublin, listens to Grattan's rebuke of Emmet, a bitterly sarcastic characterization of Emmet's 1803 rising as 'War, for the liberation of Erin!' and she interjects, 'Me four bewtyful gre-in fields. Me four bewtyful gre-in fields.' The line is a bastardization of a famous one spoken by The Poor Old Woman in Yeats's most popular play, *Cathleen ni Houlihan*, 'My four beautiful green fields,' which refers to the Irish land that must be freed from British rule. This immediately establishes the Old Flower Woman as Cathleen, the emblematic essence of Ireland, 'the traditional figure of romantic Nationalism',[13] who, when her sons take to arms to free her, is transformed from an old woman into a radiantly beautiful girl. Like Emmet's reference to the British army on Irish soil, this line sets off an involved train of associations in an Irish mind. Since Cathleen is an allegory for Ireland, her identification as the Old Flower Woman is a satiric presentation of how poor old Ireland stands in the mid-1920's — she is the 'harridan' James P. O'Reilly objected to so strongly in his letter of protest. Romantic Ireland's dead and gone but 'gap-toothed Kathleen' is still sending her poetic sons to their deaths because the I.R.A. didn't like the 1921 treaty with Britain. O'Casey's Cathleen can be an 'old snarly gob', and 'a bitch at times', Joyce's 'the old sow that eats her farrow', but neither can equal Johnston's acid satire which has turned 'matchless Kathaleen' into a whore who propositions her son's murderer as her boy lies dying. (At moments, all the women in *The Old Lady*, not the old hag alone, represent qualities of the daughter of Houlihan. The sophisticated flapper, the well-dressed woman, the two slutty young things, the lisping Maeve, the minister's wife [who also quotes Yeats's play], and, of course, Sarah Curran, are all expressionistic transformations: Ireland as she would like to be, and as she is.)

These examples, which may be multiplied by dozens more, typify Johnston's elaborate use of allusion to create controlled association. It is not unlike the method of *Ulysses* or 'The Waste Land', but Johnston insists he reached it independently.* Like

*For an excellent survey of the function of 'allusion and quotation and effects of juxtaposition' in contemporary literature, see: William York Tindall, 'Strange Relations', *The Literary Symbol* (Bloomington: Indiana University, 1955), pp. 191-236.

Joyce and Eliot, Johnston has been accused of extreme dependence upon an informed and literate audience. Hilton Edwards said of this weakness: 'It [*The Old Lady*] is marred a little by obscurity. This is the hallmark of its period. In the twenties we credited our audiences with the kind of intelligence that few among them claimed.' But Edwards concludes in tribute to the play, that in spite of its obscurity: 'the play has genuine greatness, real power to move and leaves a lasting impression.' [14] Johnston's structure may be too dense for full communication under the temporal limitations of performance and several of the play's delights may be available only on close and long acquaintance. As Micheál MacLiammoir, who has been acting the main part for over thirty-five years, has written: 'I have never played [Emmet] without finding some new aspect, some new possibility, some new problem.' [15] But there is some level on which the play communicates to every audience: the spoof of theatrical chestnuts, the violence of Emmet in quest of his ideal, the satire of Ireland. In its difficulty *The Old Lady* is a typical modern work: the deeper we penetrate into the design, the more we marvel at the artistry and enjoy and comprehend the artifact.

*   *   *

The Emmet story is the subject of many plays by Irish and Irish-American dramatists, among them Dion Boucicault, Lennox Robinson and Paul Vincent Carroll; so many that it is possible to speak of a tradition of Emmet plays and to read *The Old Lady Says 'No!'* on one level as a satire of the Emmet legend, on another as an organic continuation of that legend into the disillusioned 1920s.

'A hero of melodrama if there ever was one', Emmet is treated reverentially by the dramatists of his story — 'we all love Robert Emmet' — who accept and perpetuate only the glamorous and romantic details of his biography. In 1915, for instance, Lennox Robinson devoted one act of his Emmet play *The Dreamers* to the ludicrous truth of the actual events of the rising of 1803. But he goes on to contradict the facts in order to glorify Emmet, whose 'dream is passed on undimmed. It is being dreamed today, as vivid as ever.' [16] Emmet's legend and dream were still inspirational to Robinson a year before the rising of Easter, 1916. But the

29

fourteen years between Robinson's play and *The Old Lady Says 'No!'* were the most turbulent in Ireland's history. During that decade and a half part of the dream came true: there was Easter Week and the execution of its leaders, four years of Black and Tan War, the treaty of 1921 and Irish nationhood. By 1929, Ireland had had thirteen years of the gunman, seven of them under the Free State. The treaty had brought not peace but more bloody guerrilla warfare, this time civil war; the sons of Cathleen were frequently found in roadside ditches, a card pinned to them: 'Spies and Informers Beware!' The I.R.A. had split into Republicans and Free Staters (this odd turn of political events is satirized in the tenement scene of *The Old Lady*). The Republicans still paraded under the banner of Tone and Emmet and Pearse; revolutionary political idealism was not dead, but the machine gun had superseded the pike, the bomb was soon to come and the dream had turned sour for the forgers of the conscience of the Irish race — her artists.

Johnston packs all the agonized disillusion of his generation into *The Old Lady Says 'No!'*. He casts a cold eye on Emmet and on romantic Ireland as well:

> . . . we all love Robert Emmet. Yeats and De Valera loved him. . . . I do too; and so did Sarah Curran. . . . We all agree that it was a pity that some of his supporters had to murder one of the most liberal judges on the bench, Lord Kilwarden, and that the only practical outcome of his affray was to confirm the Union with England for about a hundred and twenty years. Our affection is not dimmed by these details. . . .
>
> The whole episode has got that delightful quality of story-book unreality that creates a glow of satisfaction without any particular reference to the facts of life.[17]

Not long before Johnston turned to the Emmet legend, other writers had begun to register the toll of politics on Ireland and Irishmen. Yeats knew that the abstract love of a cause left little room for human love. The patriot loves mankind, not men; the 'terrible beauty' of politics can 'make a stone of the heart'. Lennox Robinson had devoted the second act of *The Dreamers* to a portrait of the ordinary Irish patriot, born like Tim Finnegan with the love of the liquor, preferring the tongue as his weapon and the public

house as his battlefield. Three years before *The Old Lady* O'Casey
had caused riots with his dramatization in *The Plough and the
Stars* of the looting and tavern brawling during Easter Week,
1916. Everyone in Dublin could remember this kind of activity,
but as the Older Man tells Emmet in the shooting scene of *The Old
Lady*: 'You're not going to be allowed to hold up this country
to disgrace and ridicule in the eyes of the world. Throwing mud and
dirt at the Irish people.' The I.R.A. had also come in for its share
of O'Casey's embittered viciousness in *The Shadow of a Gunman*
and *Juno and the Paycock*. *Ulysses* was contraband in Ireland and
the average Dubliner couldn't know the 'disgrace and ridicule' of
Joyce's scatological version of the romantic legend of 'Bould
Robert Emmet, the darlin' of Erin'. At the end of the 'Sirens'
chapter, Mr. Bloom window shops at Lionel Marks's on Ormond
Quay while he digests the liver, bacon and mashed potatoes of the
Ormond Hotel:

> Bloom viewed a gallant pictured hero in Lionel Marks's
> window. Robert Emmet's last words. Seven last words. . . .
> *When my country takes her place among.*
> Prrprr.
> Must be the bur.
> Fff. Oo. Rrpr.
> *Nations of the earth.* No-one behind. She's passed. *Then and
> not till then.* Tra,. Kran, kran, kran. Good oppor. Coming
> Krandlkrankran. I'm sure it's the burgund. Yes. One, two.
> *Let my epitaph be.* Karaaaaaaa. *Written. I have.* Pprrpffrrppffff.
> *Done.*

Joyce's, the briefest and most scathing fictionalization of the
Emmet story, contains allusions that are most apposite to central
themes in *The Old Lady*. He contrasts the fine rhetoric of the
dock speech with the flatulence of Bloom, thus suggesting two
ideas: that Irish oratory and the patriotism it expresses are just
so much gas (compare with the 'pok' of the stout bottles in 'Ivy
Day in the Committee Room') and that the chasm between
Emmet's dream and martyrdom and ordinary human concerns is
absolute. Joyce also links Emmet and Christ in a very subtle play
upon the messianic longings of the Irish heroes and upon the
joyous tendency of the Irish to oblige and make martyrs of their

31

inept patriots. Read over a century and a half later, the dock speech that Joyce parodies is a compound of naive egoism and noble patriotism: '[My] ambition . . . to hold a place among the deliverers of my country will lead . . . [my] shade [to join] the bands of those martyred heroes who have shed their blood on the scaffold.' Johnston, like Joyce, captures the ironic interplay of the nobility and egoism of Emmet's motives. In *The Old Lady*, Emmet's messianic quest is updated as we follow his ironic progress through contemporary Dublin.

*   *   *

At the end of the opening playlet, Emmet is knocked unconscious as he resists arrest. The rest of the play takes place in his dream which unites in time two eras a century and a quarter apart. Appropriately, in a play conceived musically, the opening movement serves as a series of thematic preludes. The goal of Emmet's quest seems to be Sarah Curran's garden, but various allusions to him as Dante, Don Quixote, Oisin, Galahad, St. Joan and Christ; to Sarah as Beatrice and the Virgin; to Rathfarnham as the Holy Grail, the New Jerusalem, the Land of Heart's Desire, Tir Na-nOg (land of youth) and Hy Brasail (paradise) all alert us to the larger theme. For generations the pure emblem of Ireland's aspirations, Emmet is revealed as a self-appointed deliverer crying and wreaking havoc as he runs his bloody course to an illusory paradise that is death, all in the name of a beautiful dream. But Dublin, heartsick in her own way, will have none of him except as comic relief from the seedy life not ended by the bright green paint job of the Free State. Within the framework of a parody of nineteenth century melodrama intended to symbolize the perilous melodramatics of Irish politics, Johnston introduces the irreconcilable clash of dream and reality that is a central theme of the play.

The amnesiac player is thrust into busy, noisy Dublin, an abrupt scenic contrast of romantic dream and middle-class reality that marks the beginning of the play proper. From this moment on, unrecognized in an absurd uniform, Emmet is in conflict with the populace as the city is paraded before him in a series of 'epiphanies of the spirit of Dublin'.[18] The first of these is an encounter with Grattan's statue on College Green, counterpointed by the Old Flower Woman's cackling degradation of Cathleen ni Houlihan.

Grattan begins to open Emmet's eyes to the nightmare aspect of the dream: indiscriminate murder, political disaster and an eternal legacy of violence. The historical Grattan had devoted his life to winning home rule by legal means. He had written an Irish Constitution and won a voice for the Irish parliament and had lived to watch it all destroyed by the Rising of '98 which led to an enforced legislative Union with Great Britain. Emmet's 1803 rebellion only redoubled British resolve to govern Ireland from the houses of parliament. Grattan had said of Emmet's rising and execution: 'Their hanging is of little moment, but they ruin the country.' The Dubliner in the Gate audience who knew his history would appreciate the emotion of Grattan, a broken old man whose lifework was crushed by Irish patriotism, as he encountered one of those patriots: 'Full fifty years I worked and waited, only to see my country's new-found glory melt away at the bidding of the omniscient young Messiahs.'

Grattan sardonically recalls the puny rising to the self-righteous Emmet: 'Eighty tattered turncocks from the Coombe: a plumed hat and a silver sword. War, for the liberation of Erin!' Histrionic Emmet disregards non-violent Grattan and the possibility that there is more than one way to love Ireland and to fight for her freedom: 'I must go on. I must march proudly through to the final act. . . . Look! The people are waiting for me, watching for me.' Grattan's answer is the first full thematic description of Ireland as the dying land: 'Ah, the love of death, creeping like a mist at the heels of my countrymen! . . . Death is the only voice that can be heard in this distressful land.' Emmet cannot face the reality that Grattan depicts since such a recognition would mean a denial of the entire heroic mode. But the seed of doubt has been sown and the challenge delivered to Emmet's arrogant sense of mission.

Emmet's journey into disillusion continues as he becomes an onlooker at 1929 Dublin, 'Still dear. No longer dirty.' He identifies himself and begins to rally a crowd to his cause and rebut Grattan's charges: 'I will carry you away to where the spirit is triumphant. . . . Let no man blaspheme the cause that the dead generations of Ireland served. . . . Life springs from death and from the graves of patriot men and women spring living nations.' (The words are Pearse's.) Emmet in his moment of triumph, blind to the sport being made of him, is suddenly face to face with the Old Flower Woman, with the real Ireland he cannot accept anymore than he

33

could accept Grattan's derision. She too ridicules Emmet's dream:
'Ye'll be off to a better land will yez? You will . . . in me eye!'
then tells the crowd he's an imposter *playing* Emmet. The mob
turns on him, calls him a 'self-appointed instructor of the Irish
people' who will 'not . . . be allowed to hold up this country to
scorn before the world.'

The people he would save have turned upon him ('This lovely
land that . . . in a spirit of Irish fun / Betrayed her own leaders,
one by one'). A revolver is produced by a young patriot to silence
the impostor, and in order to prevent the crowd from blocking
his way, Emmet seizes it and fires. Fighting the very nation he
would redeem, rejecting their rejection of him, he mortally
wounds the young patriot. Like the opening playlet, this first part
fittingly ends in an act of violence as the play itself moves towards
Emmet's final affirmation of the value of violence. Grattan's
prophecies come true; the chain of violence in the name of the
patriotic ideal is still unriven. Ireland's talent for death is undiminished. Irish history and the national reverence for death
repeat themselves. Kilwarden had died and Emmet had denied
responsibility. Now he kills and justifies this killing as a necessary
step in the pursuit of liberty with the same words he had used to
justify Kilwarden's death to Grattan: 'What could I do? It was
war.' This scene is supersaturated with irony. The feeble gunshot,
like the rising of his eighty men, is 'war'. But this time Emmet
kills an I.R.A. lad, and the whole era of the gunman and the
Troubles is brought to mind. Emmet is still at 'war' though Ireland
is a free nation; the disaffiliated I.R.A. is still at 'war' with the
Free State and pursues a policy of random assault against an
imaginary enemy. The violent heritage of Emmet is perpetuated
into the present. The need for a cause has proven stronger than
the need for a nation.

In 1960, Johnston wrote a television play, *Operations at Killyfaddy*, in which he updated his view of the national death wish.
The play is set in 1960: the twenty-six counties are a republic
with no allegiance to Britain, yet the I.R.A. clings to the notion
that Northern Ireland is a British garrison and would end partition
by 'war' though two-thirds of the Ulster counties have not the
slightest interest in becoming part of 'the holy land of Ireland'.
In the play an I.R.A. column embarks upon a retaliatory raid
against a Big House over the Ulster border. Humiliatingly defeated

34

by the wiles of a schoolboy, the I.R.A. Commandant explains, in 1960 (not 1929; *plus ça change* . . .) the rationale of physical-force intransigence: 'Is everyone to have something worth fighting for except the young men of Ireland today? Would you have us swabbing down bars — digging for spuds — totting columns in ledgers for the rest of our lives with never a chance to shoulder a gun like them that went before us? Is it war for Ireland you'd take from us — maybe even the chance of death itself' The romance of violence is irresistible to the youth of a nation that has 'missed every great historical experience',[19] from the industrial revolution through two world wars, even though its end is not Hy-Brasail but 'death itself'.

This death scene at the end of Part One of *The Old Lady* is also a parody of the sentimental martyrdoms that abound in Irish literature of the Troubles. In Act IV of O'Casey's *The Plough and the Stars* we hear of Jack Clitheroe's 'heroic' death in Easter Week:

He was shot through th'arm and then through th'lung . . . his breath comin' an' goin' in quick, jerky gasps, an' a tiny sthream o' blood thricklin' out of his mouth, down over his lower lip. . . . I said a prayer for th'dyin', an' twined his Rosary beads around his fingers. . . . His last whisper was . . . 'I'm ready to meet my God, and I'm proud to die for Ireland." An' when our General heard it he said that "Commandant Clitheroe's end was a gleam of glory."

Johnston goes a step further in deflating Irish political martyrdom by parodying O'Casey's parody:

Older Man. Now you've done it.
Speaker. Done what?
A Voice. Oh, my God! My God!
A Man. It's Joe . . . he's got it in the breast . . .
Older Man. Joe's got it. Right through the left lung. . . .
Joe. It's welling out over me shirt boys. . . . Give me . . . I can't breathe. . . . oh, lads, I'm going . . . (as he is carried off) O my God . . . I am heartily sorry . . . for having offended Thee. . . .
Voices Lachrymosa dies illa. . . .
(*chanting*).

35

This scene, like all the scenes in *The Old Lady*, functions in at least three ways: to carry the action and characterization forward; to suggest thematically relevant associations, in this case an historical parallel between Emmet's 'war' and the present situation in Ireland; to criticize and force examination of the attitudes underlying these associations—the parody attacks the ceremonial worship of death, the martyr complex and the Irish tendency toward self-melodramatization.

In Part Two, a crescendo of unpleasant epiphanies hammers at Emmet, and he has trouble holding on to his heroic idea of himself. In an hilarious parody of an arty salon (there is even a Free State Minister for Arts and Crafts!) eager ladies implore, 'Do tell us Mr. Emmet about your wonderful experiences in the Trouble', as Grattan's statue exults at Ireland's revenge on her death-dealing patriots. Emmet's self-assurance is durable only so long as he believes absolutely in his cause, but these revelations of reality become an unbearable pressure. The soulless wasteland he sees begins to awaken him to the horrible possibility that he dreams in vain, perhaps in vanity. Desperately trying to pull himself together, he recites a collation of his speeches from the opening playlet. Following at the heels of a child's lisping rendition of 'The King's Breakfast', this recitation strips the posturing hero of all dignity. Unless he blinds himself to reality, Emmet must acknowledge he is not hero but fool. Thus threatened, for the second time he is forced to blot the scene from consciousness.

But Dublin will not leave him in peace. He is immediately accosted by an old blind beggar (a self-proclaimed descendant of Brian Boru) who embodies the degeneration of heroic Ireland. Only the blind can still affirm the heroic ideal in the face of pathetic modern-day reality. So it is fitting that the beggar should be Emmet's guide to the dark world of Dublin ('this is no city of the Living; but of the Dark and the Dead'). The seeker of paradise has wound up in a hell on earth; Cathleen ni Houlihan can no longer succour him, for she is now a disgusting hag. He is able for a moment to stop running from the revelation that has been dogging him from the start. He briefly awakens from the nightmare of history to find it is a huge joke with the laugh on him. Seeing at last through Grattan's eyes, he mocks himself:

Young Man.   Up the living Republic.

Speaker.   Up the blood-red Phlegethon. Up Cocytus, frozen lake of Hell.

Humble for the first time as he really hears the beggar's doomsday description of Ireland — 'this land belongs not to them that are on it, but to them that are under it' — Emmet battles with mute despair as Dublin strikes up a rousing wake over the corpse of the young patriot he shot. This is the shadowdance of the play's first title, where six expressionistic shadows chant the words of Yeats, Joyce, Swift, Wilde, Mangan and Shaw ('Dublin's greatest contributors to the world's knowledge of itself') to the derision of the crowd. The shadow of Emmet himself is called upon to justify his life as Dublin celebrates her own funeral in the burial of all her sons who hoped for better than she has provided. His response is a return challenge to the Dubliners of 1929 to justify what they have made of the liberty for which he fought. By the end of his journey, Emmet has seen his political archromanticism 'put into conflict with the . . . unromantic . . . facts of life'. He refuses to capitulate to these facts, his recent humility turned to scorn. His justification is a repudiation of the world as it is ('Race of men with dogs' heads. . . . I have done with you') and a final reaffirmation of his dream. This unwillingness to surrender the ideal to reality is so touching, particularly in the sordid environment in which it occurs, that it may seem Johnston has dropped the sustained irony of the play and taken sides, lining up the mocked Emmet with Ireland's jeered great writers against the 'vulgarity and waste' of modern Ireland; heralding the lyrical, 'heroic' rôle over drab acquiescence to the 'status q-oh'. But nothing in the play has prepared us emotionally or intellectually to side suddenly with Emmet. The political theme of the play cannot resolve simply into: Up Emmet! Down the Free State! after Johnston has repeatedly demonstrated Emmet's preference for death over life, for melodrama and romance over rational action. This is still the same Emmet who returned to Curran's garden to visit his beloved when he had a month to escape and regroup his forces, who can murder with a line of poetry on his lips. Throughout, a major purpose of the play has been the exposure of the obstinate vestiges of Emmetism that paralyze the nationhood Ireland so recently achieved: 'the words of dead men, the reliques of bogus tradition hold us in fetters or drive us spasmodically along vain courses.' [20] Remembering this, we might suspect a final irony in the justification scene. The peak of Emmet's heroism is no less than a self-apotheosis, the consummation of his pride and of the vanity of his messianism. Emmet calls himself 'the Word made Flesh' and declares 'I can create light. I can separate the waters of the deep.' He vows to deliver them out of the 'darkness . . . and a new world will be born out of the void'. Playing God some more, in a parody of the Ash Wednesday Commination of the Anglican Church, he curses those who oppose his martyrdom: the realists, the gradualists and the humane. The crowd, Emmet's antagonists throughout the play, join him in the praise of death, destruction, inhumanity and stupidity as they chant the responses:

> Speaker. Cursed be he who values the life above the dream. . . .
> Cursed be he who builds but does not destroy. . . .
> Cursed be he who honors the wisdom of the wise. . . .
> Cursed be the ear that hears the prayer of the dead. . . .
> Cursed be the eye that sees the heart of a foe.

Emmet and Dublin merge at last, the essential destructiveness, active and passive, of each shown forth. They deserve each other.
The Old Lady ends as it began. The actor-Emmet slowly regains consciousness and imagines he is back in Curran's garden. He believes that he has triumphed and found his personal paradise. The facts have failed to dissolve his dream or 'the immensity of his ignorance and the enormity of his self-deception' [21]: 'Ah, I was so right to go on!' He dies (the actor wakens) as he lived, convinced that Ireland 'will walk the streets of Paradise / Head high and unashamed'. The pigheadedness of this twenty-five year old lover-hero is touching but the truth of the matter is that there are no paradises on earth and have not been since Eden. And if the Free State is any indication, Ireland is not likely to be the next, though nothing less would seem to satisfy her sons.

*   *   *

If Johnston's assault on Irish political sentimentalism is effective, it will force the audience to leave the theatre with its nationalistic preconceptions shaken. Perhaps it will realize that the time has come to let the epitaphs of romance and heroism be written to make way for Ireland to join the twentieth century. There may have been an historical necessity for Emmet and Emmetism but no nation can grow up while it shuns the present for the past and the task at hand for the 'sting-a-ling-a-ling' of death and the grave's victory.

Johnston offers no way out of the political mess made by yesterday's heroes. The satirical purpose of the play is to provide the beginning of awareness that there is a mess. Johnston is too realistic and skeptical to suggest that there is a quick cure for the disease of Irish political infantilism. The first step, however, must be excision of the dead tissue of romance and melodrama in national life. It has taken Ireland forty-odd years to get on the operating table and she is beginning now to be 'a tough little, clean little, up and coming bourgeois republic'.[22] (Or, as Timothy Patrick Coogan puts it with an historian's decorum: 'She has reached a watershed in her development wherein the emphasis is no longer on political or constitutional transformation but on economic and social change.')[23] But the surgery is far from complete. If it ever should be, the political themes of *The Old Lady* will be dated.

The play still has political point and value as an attack on the destructiveness of the Irish racial myth, especially at a time when the I.R.A. can protest the government's policy of selling land to non-citizens by blowing up the farm of a German immigrant, and when events like the following still occur:

> An explosion . . . that was attributed by police to extremist saboteurs . . . believed to be members of the outlawed Irish Republican Army, rocked the manor house where Princess Margaret and the Earl of Snowden are vacationing. . . . Twenty I.R.A. men had . . . staged protest meetings against the royal couple's arrival. The town was painted with slogans saying, "Maggie, go home". . . . The I.R.A. men have stressed that they meant Margaret no harm but wanted to . . . dramatize their determination to force Britain out of the six counties of Northern Ireland.[24]

It is precisely the moral premise of *The Old Lady*, the 'ferocity of [Johnston's] Moral Positiveness'[25] that the time is long overdue for Ireland to outgrow her national death wish, to choose life over death. The ultimate source of the play's satire, power and poetry is Johnston's intense love of life and of Dublin, his 'strumpet city'. As Curtis Canfield writes, '. . . the play expresses the hope that the dead past may be buried . . . that . . . the lovers of life may prevail over the worshippers of death.' Johnston has said that 'a lot of people, foolish people, thought the play was anti-Irish'. It is no small part of Ireland's tragedy that any way to love her but unquestioning acceptance of her self-glorification is 'anti-Irish'.

THE MOON IN THE YELLOW RIVER

With his second play, *The Moon in the Yellow River*, Denis Johnston became an Abbey playwright and won an international reputation. Ironically, *The Moon* began as a spoof of the rigid formula of the 'Abbey play' in response to a joking challenge from his (then) wife Shelah Richards. Johnston started out to parody the Abbey acting style and stagecraft (in which, for instance, the first and third act sets had to be identical since the independent stagehands refused to re-set the stage after each performance). He even tailor-made the rôles of *The Moon* to conform to the types that were specialities of the various Abbey actors. As he worked on the playful material, however, the subject matter took over and the lampoon was forgotten. In its place Johnston created the best dramatic treatment we have of Ireland in the late twenties.

Like *The Old Lady Says 'No!'*, *The Moon* is a history play in the Shakespearean sense, a mixture of comic and tragic, of the heroic and the ridiculous, its purpose to show the spiritual condition of the world in a carefully ordered selection of local events. Yet no two plays so close in idea could be so opposite in mood and form. *The Old Lady* is a boisterous, indignant, ultramodern outpouring of defiance and disenchantment, a play in which, as Hilton Edwards saw, 'all that was pent up in Johnston came surging out.'[1] In contrast to the bold exclamatory mode of *The Old Lady* with its almost unbearable sharpness of satire held under massive emotional pressure, *The Moon in the Yellow River* is a probing, questioning play. After that crusading war to end war and the economic collapse of the world, after the betrayals in Irish politics of the twenties, Johnston writes a play which asks gigantic questions: What can one man do in the world, and do his actions have any meaning? What value can we embrace that will not mockingly dissolve before our eyes and leave us lonely and hopeless? *The Moon*, too, perhaps primarily, is a national play, wholly Irish. In a more realistic form that seems a retreat from the pioneering methods of *The Old Lady*, but which in its own quiet way is extraordinarily complex and delicate, Johnston mirrors the confused state of a nation. *The Old Lady* was a one-man show, an extravaganza with a prancing hero. But *The Moon* is both public and private, a play about character and relationship, about personal crisis in a political context. Its range is immense: from the traditional comic picture of the Paddy stage-Irishman and the 'Erin-a-tear-and-a-smile' view of Ireland to a tragi-farcical treatment of a passive, meditative race maladjusting to modern times. It is an 'anti-melodrama' on Irish history as well as a parable of self-discovery and personal redemption. The play clashes styles and personalities, juxtaposes the ridiculous and the real. The result is unforgettable, one of the funniest of Irish plays and one of the least sentimental. Anyone who hopes to understand Ireland in the early years of her nationhood must know *The Moon in the Yellow River*.

The Gate directors recognized that in style and stagecraft *The Moon* was more properly an Abbey play, and generously did not attempt to discourage Johnston from a début at the national theatre. This time, there were no reservations or hesitations in the Abbey's response. Johnston tells of the casual way the play was immediately accepted:

> One night Lennox [Robinson] and Mrs. Yeats came in, and I read them the first act, and they took possession of it, so to speak.[2]

Johnston expected trouble at the play's opening. He was getting used to Dublin's theatrical rows after the stir over *The Old Lady* and a humorous imbroglio over 'The Indiscreet Goat', a sacrilegious little ballet with scenario by Johnston, performed by the Gate in its Easter, 1931 *Dublin Revue* a few weeks before *The Moon* opened. Johnston, who like Joyce's Tom Kernan was 'fond of giving side thrusts at Catholicism', good-humouredly describes the japery of 'The Indiscreet Goat' which was greeted with a very small riot:

It was intended by me as offensive. It was anticlerical — a ballet with no speech in it at all. There was a farmer's boy with a flock of sheep and at the end of the flock was one goat, always slightly out of step. At certain points in Dubussy's music the goat made a little *pas seul* that ended with a somewhat improper gesture. The boy goes and gets the farmer and his family. The farmer threatens the goat but it still doesn't subsist, and they get a policeman but he can't do anything with it either. Finally, and here's where the trouble was, they get a priest, a little acolyte with a book and a candle. He exorcises the goat. There is thunder and lightning and the goat falls dead. A charming little requiem follows; the goat is covered with a shroud and they all march over the hill. At the same point in the music the goat makes the same motion — the exorcism was futile.

People in the audience rose and shouted and were thrown out. Hilton Edwards made a speech saying there was no offense meant, but there was. There was the usual correspondence in the papers. That's all there was to that.[3]

The Irish Times reported that at the moment the priest began to exorcise the goat, 'the audience was startled by a stentorian cry of "I protest! I protest against this display of irreverence!" '[4] The protestor was ejected, and subsequently wrote the customary letter to the editor, condemning the ballet as a 'caricature of a sacred Catholic rite', the precise charge that had been levelled against *The Old Lady*. The sad sequel to this inanity is that by the next night's performance, Edwards and MacLiammoir had insisted upon the removal of the 'offensive' material; the priest was converted to an inoffensive mayor and the divine ritual to the riot act. Maybe there is no theatrical censorship in Ireland because public opinion does the job more efficiently.

The Moon, though it contains a good deal of uproarious satire of Irish politics and an iconoclastic attitude toward the national image, caused no passionate reaction or denunciation as Johnston thought it might:

I had trouble with *The Moon* because it was received by the big audience of the Abbey, big compared to the Peacock, with a lot of mixed reception the first night. There was a lot of hissing and clapping and the police were there the next night. You had to sit and wait to see if there was going to be a row, but it never quite materialized, although I waited in some apprehension in the Green Room for another of those summonses to the stage that have nothing to do with a curtain call. All that it got was a rough deal from the newspapers.[5]

The Moon survived the reviewers; as Faulkner might have said, it not only survived, it prevailed. Through the years, it has been performed in five languages in cities from Poland to Australia, and has been seen on radio and television as well.

*   *   *

Of the seven plays in the collected edition, Johnston says that 'with the exception of *The Moon*', all 'are in various ways historical. That is to say, their very divergent plots have got a factual basis.'[6] While the plot of *The Moon* is Johnston's invention and has no apparent basis in fact, the play does originate in a highly topical context. Two events of the 1920's provide the points of departure for the physical action: the Free State's Shannon Scheme and the execution by the Free State in 1922–23 of seventy-seven political prisoners. Johnston combines these two historically unrelated episodes to form the forward-moving plot of the first two acts: an I.R.A. detachment attempts to launch an attack on the main power house (Johnston's addition to history) and its leader is summarily executed by a Free State police officer.

The massive Shannon Scheme (approved in 1925) was the most ambitious domestic project of the young Free State. The purpose of the Scheme was to convert the forces of the Shannon River into cheap electric power and ultimately to effect the rapid industrialization of rural Ireland. The Scheme aroused immediate and continued opposition. For the grand project, which was to take better than five years to complete, was not purely an economic plan but served also as an urgent diversionary tactic. As the Minister for Agriculture put it: 'the Government was determined to "give the people something big to think about" in the years of despondency and distrust that followed upon the establishment of the Free State.'[7] The Republicans were against the Scheme because they didn't recognize the Free State as a legitimate Irish govern-

43

ment and anything the State proposed was fair game for Republican scorn. Irish xenophobes resented the hiring of a German firm, first to determine the feasilibity of the Scheme, then to undertake its supervision. There was ideological objection to 'the cult of the machine' and the infringement of modern industry on the green countryside. Finally, there were the usual Irish theological and superstitious objections which charged the Scheme with being too ambitious — a proud transgression of human limits doomed to bring retribution down upon itself. One Irish lady, after visiting a spot where construction was under way that required the re-channeling of the Shannon, wrote in *The Irish Statesman*: 'I could not help thinking . . .that perhaps the aspiring mind of man has again over-reached itself, as at the Tower of Babel. The insulted Shannon will require a human sacrifice. Some winter's night she will rise in her wrath and sweep away this petty audacity.' [8] This rhetoric could easily have been delivered by Aunt Columba in *The Moon in the Yellow River*. Johnston saw in the resistance to the Shannon Scheme a microcosm of Ireland and he incorporated into the play all these antipathetic viewpoints as central elements of characterization and conflict.

The killing of the I.R.A. man, Darrell Blake, was suggested by a tragic irony of Irish history, the 'necessary' elimination by the government in power of former comrades-in-arms who sought to overthrow it. Johnston explains how he united both the Shannon Scheme and the 'seventy-seven dead men' into a dialectic of ideal and realpolitik:

> Although no physical assault was ever actually launched against the Shannon Hydro-electric Power Plant, a very determined effort had been made by an armed minority to make majority government unworkable. . . . This had been effectively stopped by methods equally rough, but very practical in their results . . . the recrudescence of murder as a political argument had been brought to a sudden stop by means of the counter-murder of prisoners in the hands of the new native government. . . . In the middle twenties, between seventy and eighty sincere and . . . very likeable prisoners-of-war were shot without civil trial . . . an argument that amounted to a bullet in the belly. . . . There was no legal or moral justification for such measures. . . . But the melancholy

44

fact remained that it worked. . . . This was all very sobering and disgusting. Yet it is hard to see what other answer could have been made . . . provided that we were to have any government at all.[9]

Fanciful as Johnston's use of fact may be, *The Moon in the Yellow River* is a history play, a serious interpretation of the temper of the times, of a critical moment in Ireland's destiny:

> In the early twenties, half way through a War of Independence . . . Ireland played one of her dirtiest tricks on Ireland. She refused to continue in the role of romantic villain any longer, and packed up and got out, leaving Ireland face to face with nothing but herself.[10]

Johnston's subject is ambitious. In *The Moon* he shows us a nation struggling to be born into the modern world, and, as Dobelle observes, 'the birth of a nation is no immaculate conception.' Johnston captures all the 'political, social, moral, psychological and spiritual . . . confusion'[11] of Young Ireland confronting herself alone after seven hundred and fifty years of yearning to do so. Her political idealists have not recognized that they need to be revolutionaries more than they want a country. Revolution has deteriorated into a game played to the death by the Darrell Blakes who seek a theatre in which to play the hero. These self-styled heroes must assault the Free State's industrial expansion which they fear will lead to political stability which will, in turn, wither away the last vestiges of Romantic Ireland. Yeats's report of its death and departure was grossly exaggerated.

Since national character is the source of national destiny, Johnston weaves into his dramatization of 'the Irish problem' in the twenties a concentrated, timeless image of the Irish race — all its celebrated contradictions, self-delusions, self-dramatization, ineptitude, escapism, dreaminess, superstition, irresponsibility, waste, disorder, violence, parochialism, irrationality, kindness, charm, wit, rhetoric and toughness. Although *The Moon* explored beyond the 'limited [Irish] target' of *The Old Lady* into the territory of 'international industrialism'[12] and the resistance to the passing of an old order, it is a very Irish play. Johnston sets out to use, as Joyce did, 'all the methods of an elastic art to express . . . the complicated problem of my race . . . *without* resolving it.'[13]

45

The Moon in the Yellow River is a play that presents a national state of being, not a solution to Ireland's troubles (although Tausch and Blake each have one to offer). Johnston writes a problem play, an 'anti-melodrama'[14] set in the 'dragon-ridden' days of the young Free State; a fearless play that confronts all the farce and suffering generated by the aftermath of revolution. The multiple conflicts of the drama are the irreconcilable, insoluble clashes of romantic imagination and science, man and machine, dream and reality, individual morality and necessitarian politics, 'chaos and order, anarchy and law, freedom and progress'.[15] 'The "message" of the play,' in Grattan Freyer's fine insight, 'is to reflect a genuine perplexedness',[16] to reflect the depressing fact that in 1931 'there [seemed] to be no answer' to Ireland's growing pains, her bombs and political murder, her relentless self-devouring.

*   *   *

Because *The Moon* is so multifarious in theme, so intricately modulated in pattern and so dense in ironic foreshadowing, the most reasonable way to approach it analytically is in the manner Robert Corrigan tells us we must read Chekhov: 'Begin with the opening speech and then, making cross-relationships, work through the entire play until the final curtain . . much . . as one would give a critical reading of a poem.'[17] The first act curtain opens on a set symbolic of the state of the nation. We are bombarded with images of decay, disorder, insulation. It is the Pigeon House at the mouth of the Liffey (Johnston has moved the main Shannon powerhouse from Limerick to Dublin) — isolated, 'shockingly untidy . . . the furniture worn by the sea air'; littered with remnants of armour. Beyond the walls enclosing these 'warlike relics of the past' modern civilization encroaches: the hum of the powerhouse turbines, the hoot of a ship on the river. At the outset Johnston suggests the clash of modernity with an Ireland clinging to her past — a scenic incorporation of a central conflict of the play.

Into this Irish world of chaos steps a robust vision of order and health, the German hydroelectric engineer Tausch. Tausch's reception is the antithesis of traditional Irish hospitality; he is received as a bothersome intruder although he had been invited. This marks the first of a crowd of mishaps Johnston uses to express time-honoured Irish ineptitude. Tausch's visit is ignored, the brush in his hat accidentally broken; the piano key sticks; the gunpowder is wet; Willie drops a shell; Potts's wife has drowned; a horse has been shot for no reason; Willie fails to report the arrival of Lanigan's lorries; the big gun fizzles in three attempts; and finally, by sheer accident, the grand works are razed. These pervasive farcical incidents seem to exist in the play as composites of a portrait of Irish national character and they have caused the play to be billed in England as 'a wild Irish farce'. However, the farcical moments of *The Moon*, like the farce in Ibsen or Chekhov, have a larger purpose; they are part of the play's 'profound arrangement'.[18] Many of the little accidents result in death — little Irish mistakes can have mortal consequences. Far from being a device to spoof that easy target, the stage Irishman, the farce is an indispensable part of Johnston's point of view. As Stark Young points out, 'the impression of a scene, farcical, mad, comically ironic and yet quivering with sensitive feeling and overhung with tragedy [is] the fundamental quality of Mr. Johnston's play.'[19]

In Dobelle's entrance and his initial exchange with Tausch, Johnston introduces a number of crucial themes embedded in contrasts of character and thought. Tausch assumes that he and Dobelle have much in common; they are both engineers who have dedicated themselves to the growth of under-developed countries. But Dobelle's days of commitment are over while Tausch's are in full bloom. Dobelle, 'a distinguished railway engineer', has renounced his youthful mission and has quit the outside world, choosing instead retirement to his 'hermitage'. Dobelle has admitted defeat and has accepted his and everyman's powerlessness to change the way of the world. The insoluble contradictions and the unrelievable sufferings of men, the real world and his work in it, have been relinquished by Dobelle in favour of a toy railway that runs around in circles, and quiet evenings with the unambiguous encyclopedia.

Tausch, for all his Teutonic practicality and self-professed managerial ability, is an innocent romantic. His mission in Ireland is an answer to 'the call of romance', which bids him appreciate 'the charm of the West'. Tausch's simplicity leaves him certain that all one need do to understand Ireland is take a course in her language and culture and visit a few native homes. Dobelle is amused and pained by Tausch's innocent self-assurance in a land where men 'may believe in fairies . . . but trade in pigs.' He fore-

47

sees 'with infinite pathos' the forthcoming agony of Tausch's *Irische Reise,* his encounter with 'the men that God made mad'.

Dobelle, taking pity on innocence, tries to lead Tausch through the labyrinth of Irish self-contradiction. He begins with the symbolic tale of the big gun. George (the 'Christian communist') has built the gun because 'every time the people try to be free and happy and peaceful it seems to George that somebody comes along and stops them with big guns . . . [so] he decided to make a big gun for himself so that the next time the people won't be so badly off. . . . Of course nobody knows what will happen when it's fired. But we all hope for the best.' Dobelle's account of this gun is, in the increasingly familiar Johnston manner, parabolic and rich with significant thematic overtones which depend upon knowledge of subsequent action for their ironic point. First, a gun that takes eight years to make and then doesn't work is the tragi-comedy of Ireland in little. Second, in failing to fire, this big gun stands in implicit contrast to Lanigan's little gun that does go off — an ironic contrast which suggests the whole interplay of romantic idealism and political realism. Finally, George's well-intentioned construction of a big gun to stop big guns is a parable of the cyclical nature of evil and vengeance, a theme that dominates the last act of the play. It is one of the great centres of thought in Johnston's work (we have met it before in Emmet's defense of violence and the murder of Joe in *The Old Lady Says 'No!'*).

Little in Ireland's political history is logical or rationally sequential. Mirroring this, the structure of *The Moon* exhibits no straight lines of development. Meaningful digressions are the rule. Dobelle, diverted from dire prophecy, returns to his prediction of what lies ahead for idealistic Tausch. In one of the memorable moments of Irish drama, Dobelle warns the German to get out of Ireland while he still has his energy, fed by illusion, for Ireland will not let him off with his innocence intact. She will make him confront the vanity of his idealism and pay the price of human life to bring her light:

If you stay here, you will find yourself out. . . . Here we have vampires in shimmering black that feed on blood and bombs. . . . And enormous fat crows that will never rest until they have pecked out your eyes and left you blind and dumb with terror. . . . And in the mists that creep down from the

48

mountains you will meet monsters that glare back at you with your own face.

Tausch has not yet understood a word. With a bit of wonderfully inappropriate nationalistic propaganda he offers the German solution to the Irish problem: 'Just a little organization here and you will see the change.' As the I.R.A. column that intends to destroy his 'solution' arrives outside, Tausch becomes another speechifying Messiah of Irish liberty, a light-bearing redeemer who will bring freedom through power rather than through the Irish martyr's customary 'war'. As he proclaims his mission, this well-meaning bringer of light is utterly blind to the Irish preference for mismanaging their own affairs:

> . . . freedom cannot exist save when united with might. And what might can equal electric power at one farthing a unit. I see in my mind's eye this land of the future — transformed and redeemed by power. . . . Soon you will be a happy nation of free men . . . but by the inspiration of power-power-power . . .

At this moment, as he is about to quote Horace's *exegi monumentum* (he has already pompously quoted Schiller), a comical deflation occurs, as one invariably does when the rhetoric waxes heroic. A masked I.R.A. gunman appears, for Tausch's dream of freedom through power is to be blown up that night. The terrible gunman is himself deflated from his heroic pose a moment later and then proceeds to try to convince Tausch to sell him some petrol to help burn the place down. Tausch is being treated to a grand parade of Irish illogicality, with much more yet to come. With the overwhelmed German collapsing in a chair ('I think I go mad') — the act ends as it began — nature and the outside world remain impervious to the mad goings-on.

The set of Act Two represents an incremental repetition of theme. Again we see an image of confusion and disorder and a confrontation of old and new. This act, like the first, is characterized by an immense variety of counterpointed and thematically juxtaposed movements and dialogue: anecdotes, drinking scenes, a psychological encounter, the farcical scenes of the removal of the gun and the dropping of the shell that doesn't explode, a

49

discussion of the merits of sex education for adolescent girls, an impromptu trial, a Chinese song, an execution. Of particular interest are the characterizations of Blake and Tausch, their opposing views on Ireland's salvation, Tausch's opinions of Ireland, Dobelle's opinion of Tausch and the attitudes toward progress expressed in the extemporaneous trial. We meet the I.R.A. leader Darrell Blake,

> An affable Irregular . . . [who]
> Comes cracking jokes of civil war
> As though to die by gunshot were
> The finest play under the sun.[20]

Blake makes an aesthetic of revolution ('A beautiful word. So few people appreciate beautiful words nowadays!'). He turns life into theatre and political idealism into a scenario, deluding himself that he is the dramatist and hero. The business of the evening offers Blake an opportunity to test his skill as manipulating gamester; he relishes the oncoming 'entertainment':

> This job is worthy of a bit of style. . . . Tonight I am Dick Deadeye, the boy burglar! . . . I'll give Mr. Tausch all the cat and mouse he wants and a bit to spare. . . . I'll be laughing for months. The rumble of the lorries, and the Bosch thinking he's caught us. And then bang goes the gun, up go the works to Hell, and off we trot across the sand. . . .

Insouciant Blake, generous and thoughtful, an Irishman, therefore an adept in human weakness and inconsistency, is another in the long line of irrational physical-force men who find no contradiction in killing for the sake of human dignity and spiritual advance. Blake is the inheritor of the great tradition of Irish political martyrdom pathetically reduced — with the British foe gone — to blowing up an *Irish* powerhouse. Emmet's rebellion was ludicrously executed yet grandiose in design and intent; the goal itself lent grandeur to the pitiable Rising and Emmet survived long enough to make his noble dock speech. Blake's 'entertainment' is an absurd pastiche of Emmetism — of a tradition of using violent means for changing the world, a tradition which, as Johnston made clear in *The Old Lady Says 'No!'*, must terminate since it no longer has any political justification and has deteriorated into virtually random violence. Blake would like to be in the Emmet line of Irish saviours. He accuses Tausch of playing God, yet designates himself the saviour of spiritual Ireland and Tausch the Satan of the dark mills. Blake's belief was Emmet's: death begets life, destruction saves. The four shells of the big gun are Blake's gospels: 'Four. A beautiful number. Like the gospels. Four are quite enough to save our souls. . . . If Matthew and Mark fail us, then Luke must do the trick.' As it turns out, not Luke the Healer but John the Revealer will 'do the trick' after Blake is dead without benefit of the glamour of patriotic martyrodm. And what will be revealed by the accidental explosion is that Ireland is not to be saved by the Blakes nor the Tausches.

Living at the onset of a modern age when the four green fields are beginning to sprout powerhouses, Blake needs scope for self-dramatization, an idealistic cause on which to hang his existence. A Jesuit-educated classicist, a musician, a rhetorician and a student of oriental poetry, Blake has been maimed by Irish politics. One can imagine the options open to Ireland's Blakes: the priesthood, teaching, grub street (we never *do* learn Blake's occupation) — all lives of toil at detail rarely rewarded with sudden earthly glory. 'War' is the only option left, the last arena for heroic illusions. So Blake makes war his poetics and sacrament. An 'anti-machine idealist' at a time when futuristic deification of the machine seemed to many a genuine threat to individualism,[21] Blake will destroy the destroyer of what Patrick Pearse called 'the spiritual nation'. This is the purpose he debates with Tausch as Willie and the others try to shove the gun through the door to train it on the powerhouse: 'The rest of the world may be crazy, but there's one corner of it yet, thank God, where you and your ludicrous machinery haven't turned us all into a race of pimps and beggars.' Tausch proselytizes for his beloved 'progress'; after all, even Pearse knew that 'individual happiness was partly material'.[22] In response, Blake suddenly reveals a humane idealism deeper than 'national movements'; like Yeats' Oisin, he seeks the 'three incompatible' worlds of 'infinite feeling, infinite battle, infinite repose':[23] 'If man has anything to boast of . . . surely it's his capacity for enjoying life. To me it is progress just to live more consciously and more receptively.' Tausch counters that material progress *is* freedom but Blake tells him, as Dobelle had suggested in Act One, that he is deceiving himself:

51

It's just another shackle on your limbs, and a self-inflicted one at that. I might be like you, Herr Tausch, if I choose and this country might be like yours if you had your way. But I don't choose, and you won't have your way. Because we intend to keep one small corner of the globe safe for the unfortunate human race.

An attractive argument, all the more attractive since Tausch has been behaving like the pedant of medieval farce while Blake is humane, tolerant, likeable — a poet of political idealism.

Following this crucial argument, in which Blake ironically accuses Tausch of holding immortal longings ('Tausch said let there be light, and the evening and the morning were the first day'), the act proceeds in the primary mode of the play's design with several rapid shifts of disjointed action that are carefully patterned by Johnston to reflect a nation at loose ends. After this series of shifting tempi and moods, the long-awaited Commandant Lanigan enters to arrest Blake, and Johnston brings his political motifs to the forefront. Tausch has won 'the game' and is willing to forgive and forget, but he overlooks the fact that he is an employee of the Free State and is not in a position to dispose of her 'enemies' as he wishes. He confuses his personal interest in the powerhouse with political forces too complicated for his comprehension. Lanigan reminds him that 'these works are a national affair'. From Lanigan's viewpoint the very stability of the government has been threatened and unless Blake is dealt with, the threat will recur.

The remainder of the act is a brief review of Irish history in the twenties. Blake had brought Lanigan 'into the movement in the old days, when we were all one against the British'. Blake remained a Republican; Lanigan joined the 'majority' government. (The unpopular Treaty of 1921 had been ratified by just seven votes — hardly a mandate for the Free State. Blake, therefore, as the armed representative of a significant minority, is not to be dismissed as a crank or crackpot for all his histrionics.* To fail to take him seriously is to weaken fatally the play's ideological conflict and to distort political reality.) And now Lanigan is required to execute his old compatriot, a task he does not relish.

*For a vivid account of reaction to the ratification of the Treaty, see Seán O'Casey, 'Into Civil War', *Inishfallen, Fare Thee Well*, pp. 73-83.

Blake, without knowing it, is making the final defiant gesture in a life shorn of romantic opportunity. What is to prove his death speech is an oratorical affirmation of the nationalist dream, a dream from the past that looks to the future and ignores the present reality:

> Lanigan can stop us from touching the place tonight. He can lock you and me up if he likes, and in spite of the Bosch. But he can't lock us up forever. And, as long as there's the will in our hearts the likes of him can only pollute as much of this earth as the area of their own bootsoles, so long will the future be before us.

Lanigan is the reality Blake scorns. And Lanigan's gun works: quickly, efficiently, without rancour or fanfare behind the finger on the trigger. In a wonderful stage moment, tipsy Blake is at the piano singing of the poet Li-Po who died drunk trying to embrace a moon in a yellow river (Johnston's fine image for the hopeless poetic dream of the Irish patriot who grasps at the invisible reflections of his drunken visions). Tausch is impatiently carping about Irish gab and do-nothingness: 'Here you will talk a lot but it comes to nothing. You and your guns that will never fire. This is no country. It is a damned debating society. Everybody will talk — talk — talk. But nothing ever happens.' This almost Chekhovian mixture of two people wanting utterly different things from life, exposing themselves unheeded, is suddenly punctuated by the most effective and arresting action in all Johnston's plays. In starkest contrast to the genial and unhurried stage-Irish business that concluded the previous act, Lanigan shoots Blake without a word. No Emmet-style romance and hiding in the hills for Darrell Blake; no hushed courtroom with an artist capturing images for eternity; no immortal dock speech; no public execution and martyrdom. Just 'a bullet in the belly' (or in the back, in some productions) that brings all the 'talk — talk — talk' down 'from the plane of abstract speculation to the reality of blood and death.'

Act Three has a double focus: on Tausch's inability to accept any responsibility for Blake's death and on the effect of the evening's strange events upon Dobelle. To avoid confrontation with the unacceptable lesson of the shooting — that there is no progress without destruction and every step forward must be taken over a corpse — Tausch accuses Lanigan of 'murder'. Utterly confident in the rectitude of his moral code, according to which all problems have solutions — *his* solutions — Tausch applies fixed principles to an intractable reality that refuses to yield to his or any man's 'principles'. Lanigan, on the other hand, is the total political realist. He was a Republican who joined the Free State police and now has to slaughter his old friend, a painful job that must be done, given the condition that the Free State must defend itself. And he knows where all this will end for him — some Republican like Willie Reilly will revenge Blake:

> I'm only doing my job — the job I'm able to do — the job that always seems to deliver the goods. . . . When I took on this job I said to myself: "Well, I'll last as long as God allows me!". . . . I suppose you think I enjoy [it] when it means a bullet in my own back sooner or later. . . .
> I only hope that when my time comes I'll be plugged fair and clean like he was. . . . And I believe that if ever I meet him again he'll bear me less ill-will for what's finished and done with, than those that are left behind. . . .
> I'm a gunman. I always was and I always will be. . . . But God help you all if I wasn't. . . . They'll not touch this powerhouse again! . . . Whatever happens now will be a personal matter between me and the likes of Willie Reilly.

That the necessity for the survival of the state is beyond morality is no news since Machiavelli, despite Irish Mitchel's 'There are some things a man must not do to save his country.' But the pity of it! Unless one takes a Marxist view like that of the reviewer of a Warsaw production of *The Moon*: 'Lanigan, representing the point of view of the author, states that a revolution must, when successful, destroy those who created it.' Lanigan goes a step farther; he knows that there is no end to the cycle of destruction. He has killed the British; he has killed Blake; he will be killed for killing Blake; his killer will be killed in turn . . . and no end, always for reasons that seem justifiable: the state is crushing the spirit (Blake's), the state must survive (Lanigan's), justice must be done (Tausch's), and so on.

Lanigan knows he is part of an unending cycle but Tausch does not. Tausch seeks Dobelle's approval of his decision to turn

Lanigan in for Blake's death, but Dobelle refuses to take any part in denouncing Lanigan. Bitterly depressed over the hopelessness of history, Dobelle tries to force Tausch to see his rôle in this cycle of vengeance, for Tausch is about to make his second phone call of the evening, one that will result in Lanigan's death, as the first resulted in Blake's. Recognition of the 'monsters that glare back at you with your own face,' — that *we* are history — is the only hope of breaking the chain of violence. Dobelle's refusal to continue the chain does not mean that 'the folly of vengeance' will end. All one man can do is act out of awareness of the probable consequences of his choice and refrain from playing any part in the perpetuation of evil. Dobelle explains to Tausch the moral rationale of his refusal:

Hanging [Lanigan] won't bring back Blake. . . . I prefer to continue hating him. Lanigan? . . .
Lanigan is just yourself. He is your finger on the trigger. Denounce him by all means. The tribute to your works is not yet complete. For if he doesn't hang for Blake then Willie will hang for him, and I'm sure you'd like to save Willie. . . . Two more lives, Herr Tausch, but what of it! In this welter of blood one great factor will be borne in upon us. The works will remain. Man may perish, but they have been saved.

Lanigan's prosecution, of course, will have nothing to do with the survival of the works. His punishment will simply reflect Tausch's personal belief that 'all guilt must be avenged on earth'.

But Ireland will not let Tausch off with a mere tongue lashing. He launches into a peroration of his ideal of a perfectly ordered, forward moving universe: 'Everything you see has its purpose in the scheme of things. . . . Look down at the works. What do you see? . . . The great river . . . the turbine house beside the old slag heap. Everything with a purpose.' At this very moment the shell that George and Potts have tossed on the slag heap explodes and the works are 'Blown to hell. Pure accident' — the final absurdity. Blake has been defeated, killed in the name of the works which couldn't be saved. Now Tausch is defeated and another link is added to the chain of violence and revenge: 'Brutus is avenged, O Octavius', Dobelle cries out. Ireland repudiates both her saviours, the dreamers Blake and Tausch; the only light she will have now until Tausch can rebuild the powerhouse and another Blake try to blow it up is the dawning sunlight that begins to mingle with the glow of the powerhouse fire.

As far as the political action of the play is concerned, the cycle of death and destruction is complete. But the play is not over. It does not end on this note of despair. Blake, the mystical revolutionary who doesn't know which end a gun fires from, has played out his pointless drama of patriotism; Lanigan the gunman has performed his ugly duty; Tausch, the well-meaning fool, has discovered a world he will never understand nor manage. Without seeing the paradox, he believes still that his dream for 'the future of humanity' is 'greater than the life of man'. Of the four major characters Dobelle alone salvages something from this night of farce and terror.

Throughout the play, Dobelle, his heart grown brutal from the early death of his wife in childbirth and the loss of his youthful Tausch-like faith in human progress, vents his disappointment in 'sarcastic' scoffing at the public world and the personal dream — the illusions of progress or spiritual fulfillment for which men die. As the night ends, Dobelle makes explicit his credo of denial which applies both to Church and progress, but in a vocabulary newly freed of invective, cleared of bitterness, and in praise of life:

> I'm not against their [Catholic] religion. I'm against their rightness. It is right that a women should die so a child's immortal soul should be saved from Limbo, therefore I say that I'm against right. It is right that men should murder each other for the safety of progress. I admit it. That is why I am against right and believe in wrong. When I look back over my life, it's as plain as a pikestaff to me. It's always evil that seems to have made life worth while, and always righteousness that has blasted it. And now I solemnly say that I believe in wrong, in the misery that makes man so much greater than the angels.

This acceptance of evil and death, of violence and suffering, of life with all its painful incomprehensibility, is the cornerstone of a theology that Johnston is to elaborate upon over the years. In 1954, Johnston wrote of *The Moon*:

Looking at it again, after rather more than twenty years, two things strike me about it: first how strange it is that so much of what one finds out subsequently to be true can go into a play written at a comparatively early age. Second, how little critical comment was evoked on what it really is about.

(Johnston refers to the view of the play as a melodrama of heroes and villains, victims and victimizers, or as a 'wild Irish farce'.) In a group of sermons delivered in the nineteen fifties at Mount Holyoke and Smith Colleges, Johnston dealt in detail with a 'philosophy of life' already embraced in *The Moon* and reinforced by his response to the history of Europe in the thirties, the second World War, the Nürnberg trials* and the thermonuclear arms race:

> For a good many years I have been puzzled by religion's failure to give me an answer for the paradox of Good and Evil — the existence of pain and misery . . . the inevitability of violence and struggle as a part of the fabric of life itself, while religion preaches Peace.

He concludes that:

> If there is misery in this world — and there is — it is also the thing that makes us conscious of happiness. . . . The incomprehensible [is] the only thing that man can really understand.

Dobelle, in 1931, gives voice to this philosophy. He is forced by the death of Blake into a self-confrontation from which he emerges longing for the capacity to pity the Irish and human conditions and for the ability to give up his 'cursed gift of laughter'. Both Blake and Tausch sought a utopian happiness, but Dobelle realizes that 'it is only men who can really be unhappy. And yet isn't it unhappiness that makes men so much greater than the trees and the flowers and all the other things that can't feel as we do?' He

---

*In 1947, Johnston reaffirmed his abhorrence of the vicious cycle of vengeance in a letter to *The Times*, London, 16 May, 1947, protesting the death sentence given to Kesselring: 'If the execution of prisoners is a criminal offense, against which Kesselring ought to have protested, it is no less incumbent upon us to protest the execution of Kesselring.' Compare this to Dobelle's reason for not turning in Lanigan.

looks on death and is shocked out of his self-pity and isolation into a beginning of love for his long-estranged daughter. In the insane world of affairs there can be only a cycle of vengeance and destruction to which 'there's no solution'. But in the private world there is hope for order and decency. A man can, as Dobelle does, deny a part in the cycle, transcending vengeance to make a separate peace by accepting life as it is.

With Blake and the works lying dead, the 'morning starts to shine' and word is received that after a three-day labour a child is born to a neighbour; death and devastation, love and birth, and a ray of hope through acceptance. Life goes on in joy and agony, irreducible to any man's plan for it, and the play ends as it began, with Agnes in charge and the ship hooting in the river.

Critics have charged *The Moon* with ending twice, the last scene being a sentimental 'conversion worthier of Richard Steele than Denis Johnston'.[24] When we remember that the beginning of Dobelle's personal redemption is wrested out of death, despair and disillusion and in no way implies political optimism, it seems less a 'conversion' than a realistic recognition of the only meaning life can still hold for him. And it is balanced if not overshadowed by his political skepticism: 'Darkness . . . death and darkness. Ah, can anything cure *them*? . . . I wonder' Not a 'conversion' at all, Dobelle's return to life is one man's and only one man's decision that in a world of unending disorder, or at the best disorder with no end in sight, a man can only make sense of chaos by accepting it and trying to put his own house in order. Curtis Canfield goes too far in finding more than this personal hope in the final action:

> The works are ultimately destroyed by accident and thus both antagonists are defeated. The wasteful, blundering land, . . . is the final victor. . . . Ireland can take care of herself. Unchanged, unchanging, she looks serenely down on a new day as a ship hoots merrily in the yet unsullied Shannon; and out of her immensity she gives a new life as if to prove Blake's was as nothing compared to her abundance. Agnes, the old Mother, the symbol of Ireland . . . contradicts Dobelle's gloomy prophecy about Death and Darkness by announcing the birth of the latest Mulpeter and by letting the light stream in through the window.[25]

Very comforting! but a national sentimental conversion that is the antithesis of Johnston's and Dobelle's question, to which 'there is no answer and you know it'. Dobelle's life has a future, but 'the Irish problem' remains just that. Denis Johnston, meditating on Ireland's civil war, comes to Yeats's uncomfortable conclusion: 'We are closed in and the key is turned on our uncertainty.'

A BRIDE FOR THE UNICORN

Before he was thirty, Denis Johnston had written two of Ireland's finest plays, *The Old Lady Says 'No!'* and *The Moon in the Yellow River*. Although antithetical in method, in subject they are companion plays, passionate entreaties to reason and clarity. On the surface anti-heroic, their complaint is not against an heroic idea — there is too much undisguised affection for Emmet and Darrell Blake for that — but against the specific results of heroic idealism at a definite point in Irish history. In another place at another time these brave and gifted young men would be shining knights; but in the Free State which had known little except perpetual 'violence on the roads', they had to be renounced. The tension and force of these two plays are rooted in Johnston's control of a pervasive sympathy for the poetic impulse and the grand gesture; the man of law oversees the poet, the political intelligence checks the visionary. Both plays exhibit the essential qualities of his best work: great natural theatricality, intricate structural complexity, a witty and ironic anti-sentimentalism and an intense belief that life must be lived to the hilt. All these are again prominent in his third play, *A Bride for the Unicorn* (1933), a highly personal play about how to be, how to love, and how to die.

The reader coming from Johnston's 'paradox island'[1] in the first two plays is immediately struck by the un-Irishness of *Unicorn*. Freeing himself in this play from total immersion in his Irishness, Johnston lets loose all the sensitive lyricism and love of life implicit in the earlier works. He moves into a subjective field of vision and a private mythology captured in a free-floating time and memory form as different from *The Old Lady* and *The Moon* as they are from each other. *Unicorn* is his most original experiment (not like the *Old Lady* tied to a genre such as expressionism); in fact 'one of the most original pieces of dramatic technique in the Irish drama'.[2] And perhaps because he leaves the steadying framework of Irish

59

history behind as he heads for new territory in trying to dramatize what means most to him, *Unicorn* emerges as the least controlled though most ambitious of the three, for it is Johnston's *Finnegans Wake*, no less than an effort to capsulize all history and mythology into the story of an everyman. But he has never been able to generate a form which can both contain such dense material and communicate successfully to an audience in a theatre. Although it was for many years his favourite among his plays, Johnston recognizes its unsolved problems. He regrets having published it prematurely in 1935 and considers it still a work in progress. Alone of his important plays it was excluded from the collected edition. Johnston is a meticulous craftsman, and as we have seen in *The Old Lady* and shall see again, an 'inveterate reviser'.[3] He explains his hesitation about *Unicorn*, which he has been rewriting intermittently for thirty-five years:

> My plays seem to resemble those racing cars that appear at one event in a certain condition, at the next with a different engine, and at a third with quite a new body. And if they get into print before this fascinating progression runs down either through boredom or from lack of further inventiveness, they haunt me afterwards on the bookshelves of my friends, like those disturbing photographs of oneself at a different age that should not be allowed. This is why I do not like them to be printed too soon — as has happened to my favourite play (not my best known), the published version of which I now dislike quite violently.[4]

Hilton Edwards's remarks on *Unicorn* comprise a typical dual reaction to the play: an awareness of weaknesses in structure, and especially in characterization, with an appreciation of its 'boldness and grandeur':

> In *A Bride for the Unicorn* the perfection of structure [of *The Old Lady Says 'No!'*] is shattered. It becomes cumbersome and overcomplex . . . relying for its efficient performance upon mechanical appliance, rostra, steps and swift scenic changes, and even requiring for complete representation a revolving stage. . . . The central character . . . is an abstraction, not a living character. But in spite of all this, . . . *A Bride for the*

60

Unicorn is a grand play. . . . What a thrilling play to produce, and what a brute![5]

Johnston's own reservations sanction fault-finding; but whatever the faults of the play in its present published form, *Unicorn* remains a significant revelation, not of dead ends, but of ripening themes whose beginnings we have encountered in *The Moon in the Yellow River*. In maintaining his affection for *Unicorn*, Johnston was not just a frustrated parent indulging his most recalcitrant offspring. For *Unicorn* is the first of Johnston's plays to incorporate a full dramatic statement of 'the philosophy of life that is at the back of most of what I write'. In *Unicorn*, Johnston leaves Ireland to voyage into an exploration in human time and to dramatize the mature evolution of the philosophy that Dobelle began to grope for at the end of *The Moon in the Yellow River*. The expression of this philosophy involves Johnston in the dramatization of a complex metaphysic of time as well as in an attempt to present with the force of myth the cycle of human life and death and man's struggle to wrest meaning out of chaos and identity out of the fear of extinction. As William York Tindall writes: 'this queer play . . . pursues ideas of love, time and death. Doing this, it creates a myth by the aid of myths.'[6] The themes of *Unicorn* are rooted in a complicated structure that interweaves mythological allusion, parallel and parody with a theory of time and ethics.

*   *   *

'What the devil hast thou to do
with the time of day?'
1 Henry IV

On its surface, *A Bride for the Unicorn* tells the story of John Foss, a shy schoolboy who spends a mystical night of passion with a masked lady, his spiritual bride, who disappears after their nuptial night. He lives the rest of his life on two planes: the mundane rhythm of marriage, responsibility, disappointment, death; and the superstructure of a perpetual quest for his lost bride who endures in memory as the symbol of complete fulfillment, a consummation itself symbolized by a rose that remains on stage throughout the play, in stark contrast to the angular monochromes

61

which represent the limits and pressures of daily life. The simultaneous double existence in the ordinary and in memory of the sublime, coupled with the multi-mythical parallels in the quest-journey, make for almost inextricable formal entanglements. Hilton Edwards points out that *Unicorn* is 'a development of the symphonic form used in *The Old Lady*. It has a dominant plot or motif, with secondary and tertiary themes, unfolding not alternatively in the manner of plot and sub-plot, but simultaneously in the manner of counterpoint.'[7] The main source of the play's extraordinarily difficult construction is Johnston's desire to embody in the story of an everyman his ideas of the nature of our life in time.

Questions of the nature of time in relation to ethical, moral and psychological behaviour, always primary in literature, become in contemporary literature — heir to Bergson, Freud, James and Einstein — a 'preoccupation . . . a predominant theme'.[8] The pioneering of Proust, Joyce and Virginia Woolf into realms of time and consciousness during the first three decades of the twentieth century had, by Johnston's time, become part of the standard technical equipment of the modern writer. Many writers of the thirties suspended between two wars — Johnston and J. B. Priestley are representative — began to search (with well-learned lessons from the masters in stream of consciousness and surrealist techniques) into 'the time problem' for a new humanism and new intimations of immortality. As Priestley wrote in 1937:

> This problem of Time was the particular riddle that the Sphinx had set for this age of ours . . . it was like a great barrier across our way and we were all squabbling and shouting and moaning in its shadow, and if it could be solved there might follow a wonderful release and expansion of the human spirit.[9]

In 1929, the English aeronautical engineer and philosopher J. W. Dunne published what he considered to be a final solution to the problem of Time in a book called *An Experiment with Time* which very rapidly became extraordinarily popular: 'This theory [Dunne's] has become as much a part of an undergraduate's first year equipment as a selection of bow-ties.'[10] Johnston read and responded to Dunne, and Dunne's theory is at the centre of

Johnston's thought and construction in *A Bride for the Unicorn*.

Dunne's theory of time, known as Serialism, posits the simultaneous co-existence of an infinite series of time dimensions. In our ordinary waking state we perceive 'time as a zip fastener which closes behind us, leaving the past irrevocably fixed, while what is yet to come lies undetermined before us,' [11] *i.e.*, the traditional Newtonian view of temporal progression in which the present the next moment becomes the past and the future the present. Dunne calls this Time 1. He observes, however, that we are conscious of our behaviour in Time 1 and we cannot be both observer and actor at once. Therefore, our time sense, or consciousness of our existence in Time 1, must be in some way beyond Time 1. To support this contention, Dunne introduces what he terms an 'empirical' conclusion. He became a statistical recorder of his dream-life and grew certain (after sending out questionnaires to acquire significant data from other dreamers) that dreams predict the future as often as they recount the past. The absorbing narrative of his researches comprises the bulk of *An Experiment with Time*. For Dunne's hypothesis about dreams and the future to be true, the dreaming consciousness must perceive Time 1 as an 'eternal present', a totally apprehendable spatial dimension. The dreamer then operates from what Dunne calls Time 2 and from there can see all of Time 1. Time is usually considered beyond space, the fourth dimension. But to Dunne, Time 1 is precisely a fourth spatial dimension when seen from the vantage point of Time 2, the fifth dimension. The faculty observing our ordinary time span Dunne calls 'the Ultimate Observer' for it sees all our linear life spatially. It follows that more than one dimension of time functions continually. We are always aware too that the fifth dimensional observer is at work, so there must be a sixth time dimension to which Time 2 appears spatial. And so on: for Dunne, time is an infinite regress which can, like any infinite regress, be entirely described by its first two terms.

This theory, which Dunne elaborates in four books, with mathematical 'proofs', has numerous loopholes.* However, its logical validity is irrelevant here; what matters is that Johnston found a number of the implications of Dunne's formulations con-

*For a thorough critique of Dunne, see: M. F. Cleugh, *Time* (London: Methuen, 1937), pp. 166-188.

genial to his own thinking and he used Serialism as a main building block in the construction of *A Bride for the Unicorn*. The play repudiates man's fear of death:

> . . . the theme, as succinctly as I can put it, is this: every man believes that he is afraid of death. That is not so: if he were really afraid of death he would refuse to grow up or develop in any direction. He would remain a Peter Pan all his life. For the more vital we are and the more vitally we live, the more inevitable we make our death.[12]

Dunne offers a mathematical, not a supernatural basis for a 'new immortality'. If consciousness exists in a fifth time dimension beyond the 'end' of our future and another observing self exists in a sixth time dimension to which the entire fifth dimension is visible, and so on; that is, if at the end of the first term in an infinite time series we reach the beginning of the second and at the end of the second the beginning of the third . . . then, in the phrase Dunne used as the title of his last book, 'nothing dies'. Serialism, Dunne maintains, is no less than 'a scientific argument for human immortality' in the form of a deathless consciousness'. All talk about 'death' or 'immortality' has reference to *time,* and is meaningless in any other connection. But a time system is a regressive system, and it is only in the lop-sided first term of that regress that death makes its appearance . . . in second term time we individuals have beginnings, but no ends.'[13] Whatever its logical validity, the theory offers an alternative to the pessimistic materialism Dunne felt was inundating man's spirit — a mathematical argument for temporal immortality. Dunne implies 'an immortality without the necessity of a deity, and therefore without the need for a faith combined with religious practice and doctrine. [It] provides, for the romantic sceptic, the comfort of an eternal life with apparent scientific justification . . . [and has] enormous and optimistic emotional appeal.'[14]

Fortunately, Denis Johnston did not write *A Bride for the Unicorn* solely as an illustration of Dunne's time theory. The life of the main character, Johnston's everyman, John Foss, is an adventure in consciousness that ends, *not begins,* with John's realization that only his body will die, and this comfort comes only after he has known the fear and trembling of imminent oblivion.

John Foss discovers Dunne after he nearly succumbs to anxiety and doubt generated by his battle against obliteration in Time 1. The play is not a static unfolding of a system, but the story of a dynamic inner struggle against despair, a painful and lonely quest for meaning. Johnston's urgent theme insists that modern man must seek his heroism not in flamboyant action but in the hard-won vision that denies the absurdist idea of the ultimate meaninglessness of life.

A Bride for the Unicorn opens with a comic prologue in heaven; determined to give us an everyman play, Johnston begins it in the traditional Faustian way. The prologue requires careful explication, since it is incomprehensible without knowledge of Dunne. A stationary pendulum and a handless clock at once focus our attention on matters of time. We are in an 'aery timeless region' (outside the Time 1 existence of John) where all the possibilities of Time 1 coexist. This Time 2 realm is presided over by an 'Ultimate Observer' (Johnston dramatizes as a separate character what in Dunne is an aspect of the individual) who distributes the already completed script of John's Time 1 life — the whole that John will only live in fragments. The script is a 'musical composition' without time notation. Following Dunne, Johnston employs an extended musical analogy for the time theory. The wide varieties of music in the play, with two kinds frequently overlapping, function not only to create mood but also as reinforcing modes of expressing the time themes; throughout the play 'music [is] intimately connected with the plot.' For example, a jazzy Time 1 dance will be heard among the strains of leitmotif musical themes from the Time 2 world of the prologue, suggesting that Time 1 exists wholly within Time 2. Parallel to the use of music, the staging and design of the original Gate Theatre production of 1933 tried to suggest two time dimensions encompassing the play's action. The stage was divided into three playing areas: the usual stage level, a ramp which led to the third area, and a raised platform. Any of these areas could be used to symbolize different but simultaneous time realms. MacLiammoir's curtain, with a harsh metropolis at the bottom under a flying unicorn and a floating masked lady, also underscored two regions of consciousness, the earthbound and the soaring.

Once the celestial prelude initiates a mood of mysterious expectation, John Foss is symbolically born into life by an act of sexual love with a masked lady who enters out of the clock. When he accepts the woman he begins to live; the pendulum is set swinging, the clock which now has hands strikes midnight and John is in Time 1. John enters a moving present that must end with the body's death. But there are compensations: he will be granted a glimpse into the eternity of Time 2 through the sexual communion that is the body's life. These two hours in Time 2 will leave John a memory of 'a time behind Time' and a sense of an existence in a dimension beyond the dull agony of the daily round. Yet the memory will also torment him with an exacerbated sense of the emptiness of living in Time 1 alone — he will have to go to the end of his journey to recapture the tantalizing reality of Time 2.

Johnston chooses an ideal sexual experience, a moment of total intimacy and self-realization, for Foss' sojourn in Time 2. This consummation changes John utterly ('Pendantries must shiver in the hall / When dreams are put to bed'); from the timid, celibate adolescent literally buried in books, listening to the Song of Solomon outside his schoolroom window on Christmas Eve ('Life is a voice in the street'), he is transformed into a zestful, self-assured young man: 'Something has happened to me. . . . I have seen beauty, fierce and unashamed. One night has changed the colour of all nights. . . . She has endowed me with an eighth sense and now I have become a very fierce and terrible man.' This eighth sense is a sense of Time 2 and John's Time 1 will from this point on be overshadowed by a dimension in which he feels he has been his real self. Time 1 will frequently seem but a dream to him as he moves toward death and reawakening into Time 2.

'The first moment of [John's] life' is no sooner lived than lost. He has been granted but a foretaste of immortality; now he sets out, accompanied by the Seven Companions (his schoolmates), on his quest for his lost bride — a journey into life and self-discovery. The revolving stage spins John and the Companions through the cycle of life from midnight to midnight, Christmas to Christmas, birth to death.

The first scene of this quest, 'The Rape of the Spring Goddess', also depends heavily upon Dunne. John is with Egbert and while the actual time continues from the previous scene, a good deal of time also seems to have elapsed. (Egbert the Eccentric, in contrast to the other six Companions who live only in the Time 1 world of stock response, self-interest and cliché, has an obscure connection

66

with Time 2, appearing at times a surrogate for the absent bust, the Ultimate Observer. He alone understands John's loss of the Masked Lady and weeps while the rest crack dirty jokes; the others carry Time 1 watches but Egbert carries an incongruous alarm clock that goes off at random as a parody of the rigidity of Time 1-bound life.) The action seems to be unfolding both chronologically and as memory and prospect — what is happening has happened and will happen. The multiple time perspectives, or the sense of all times as an 'existing now' presents no obstacle to the student of Dunne. The love scene with Doris too is both immediate event and memory; Dunne's time permits Johnston to dramatize the dreams of youth and the disappointments of maturity alongside each other, without chronological progression. It is impossible to unravel the 'now' of this scene, whether John and Doris are 'in' the present looking back at the past or in the past looking at the future. Insofar as this complex intermingling of time dimensions is dreamlike, the technique of *Unicorn* may be called *surrealistic*, not limiting that classification to images of blue-haired revolvers or slit eyeballs but taking it in the wider context of dream and wakefulness as a continuum. The surrealists were also concerned with the interaction of dream states and waking consciousness, each 'contributing to each other's intensity', neither being a contradiction of the other, nor, as in Freud, is the dream a less defensive, deeper reality.[15] Surrealism would have welcomed Dunne had he written twenty years earlier. The sense of interpenetration of dream and reality, or, more accurately, the interpenetration of two levels of temporal reality, pervades *A Bride for the Unicorn* and creates an atmosphere of vague mystery very appropriate for Johnston's everyman time-traveller who doesn't quite know where or when he is.

As Time 1 passes, John loses the vividness and succour lent by his memory of the 'enigmatic moment' he spent in Time 2. The spiritual sustenance gained from his sexual initiation by the Masked Lady is still potent in his enormous vitality and cockiness in Scene V, where he seduces Doris, but begins to fade into the panic of entrapment in Time 1. In Scene VII, John and Doris have been married several years; the romance of youth has eroded into the battle of the sexes. Once again, temporal distinctions are blurred in this scene, the most emotionally intense in the play. While John has loved, married, procreated and stopped loving, the quest for the lost lady progresses on another plane of consciousness. Though the quest is actually an interior journey—John's discovery of Time 2 within himself — throughout the play Time 1 (John's waking self) and Time 2 (the world of the quest and the Ultimate Observer, the Bust) are treated as equally real. Until John earns the revelation of Time 2 within himself, Johnston dramatizes it as an external entity, in conflict with Time 1. The theatrical reification of Time 2 makes this a play and not a lecture. Thus, while John is embroiled in vicious, mechanically repetitive marital squabbling (dramatized in a catechistic style borrowed from the 'Ithaca' episode in *Ulysses*) the radio broadcasts the voice of the Bust announcing the progress of events among the Companions' quest for the Masked Lady. Time 2 is ever-present, though in the dreary process of everyday living John begins to lose sight of it, and despair.

John's desperation reaches its peak in the phantasmagoric eighth scene, 'Pandora's Box', which has been accurately likened to the 'Circe' episode of *Ulysses*. The bar-room habitués suddenly shift into fantastic projections of John's frustrations and anxieties; the significant people in John's life — nanny, priest, wife — return in a *danse macabre* of accusation and recrimination. The Time 1 clock ticks loudly as John seems to have abandoned all hope of Time 2 and runs from his own shadow, 'the Fear of Death': 'The years wrap round me like a winding sheet and hope dies in my eyes. I can see nothing but mortality.' On the brink of capitulating to his despair, John summons the memory of the Masked Lady, his *ewig weibliche,* and smashes the Time 1 clock, much as Stephen Dedalus shatters Bella Cohen's lamp.

With time scrambled as usual, John soon finds himself in battle ordered to kill an enemy who turns out to be Egbert (Scene X). This scene is crucial thematically, for it is here that Egbert reveals Dunne to John. More importantly, Egbert emerges as a spokesman of the playwright's 'philosophy of life' which develops the ethical implications of Dunne's immortality. Egbert is unafraid of death for he knows that death 'is a good thing'; it is the beginning of Time 2 in which 'we will all each have our own world', where all Time 1 still exists. Because it does not die, life must be lived as fully as possible (or we would truly be left with nothing); all of its agonies and 'endings' embraced joyfully. In Dunne's (and Egbert's) metaphor life is a song that can be as simple or as rich and complicated as the singer makes it. Egbert says:

68

When the singer has sung, are his notes dead? Whatever has been, will be, while Time remains. You would not wish to sprawl through endless space. Why then be bothered that we terminate in Time? . . . Maybe our lives are nothing but a tune played by somebody upon a piano.

To which John replies, 'Then we would certainly be immortal.' John accepts contradiction and pain as well as pleasure and joy as the human condition and lives out the remaining events of his life in Time 1 with renewed exuberance.

Egbert's initiation of John into the mystery of Dunne places us at the crux of Johnston's thought. Life must be lived intensely and accepted as it is, an interwoven fabric of joy and pain, peace and evil, for 'without contraries is no progression', according to both Blake and Johnston. The following verses from Blake's 'Auguries of Innocence' could well stand as an epigraph to Johnston's canon:

> It is right it should be so;
> Man was made for Joy and Woe;
> And when this we rightly know
> Thro' the World we safely go.
> Joy and Woe are woven fine. . . .

'This', Johnston writes, 'is the counsel of contradiction',[16] in which man should rejoice. Everyman's quest — John Foss' and Johnston's own in his World War II autobiography, *Nine Rivers from Jordan* — is a passage through innocence and experience to redemption in the form of 'a love of life and an extraordinary joy in everything . . . an innocence beyond maturity.' [17]

In Johnston's view, the ability to live meaningfully depends upon an awareness of the futile repetition of Time 1 events, an awareness that creates opportunity for change and growth. When Foss refuses to kill Egbert he, like Dobelle in *The Moon in the Yellow River*, breaks a chain of vengeance:

'Why should I kill to save the scheme of things?'

The Acolyte in *Nine Rivers from Jordan* tosses his gun away; Palliser in *The Scythe and the Sunset* chooses a quiet death over a martyrdom that would require revenge: again and again the character who represents the centre of value in Johnston's work abjures a cycle of evil, a choice which empowers him to accept life joyously and to meet death fearlessly, like a bridgegroom embracing his bride.

All this has little to do with Dunne, outside of the proposition that life endures and therefore should be lived intensely, lest the memory be of nothing. The cycle of vengeance and the individual maturity that rejects it, ideas that dominate Johnston's thought from his earliest work, are close to some tenets of P. D. Ouspensky, a mystical Russian time theorist whose work Johnston also knew.* Ouspensky, in *A New Model of the Universe*, which also enjoyed a vogue in the early thirties, propounded a cyclical theory of eternal return, a 'time circle'. Some lives, however, move not in a circle but along a spiral track; granted insight into the nature of the time cycle, these lives can move beyond repetitive evil and mankind can evolve morally, very slowly, as a result of individual choices. John matures in *Unicorn*; all the others age without changing: Lewis the Loving is a perpetual lecher; Albert never stops walloping his fellow thief Harold; Dora is twice fired from jobs for clumsiness, and so on. The character who escapes the hell of eternal sameness and in so doing holds open the hope that his actions can reverberate in the world of affairs is the Johnston hero — Dotheright of *The Golden Cuckoo*, the autobiographical journalist of *Nine Rivers from Jordan*, John Foss in this play.

In the final scene of *Unicorn*, as we might expect, the journey ends in lovers meeting, and John discovers that his 'bride', the Masked Lady, is Death, the price we pay for the privilege of living. Our life in Time 1 has meaning only *because* it ends. Death is not only peace, it is the triumphant beginning of understanding. Johnston believes that death makes the whole of life available to us and gives it shape:

'Save us, O Phoebus, from the fear of Endings.'

John, who has learned this wisdom and teaches it to us, is carried off to a hero's burial.

*I found densely annotated editions of the works of Dunne and Ouspensky on Johnston's bookshelves in Northampton, Massachusetts.

Dunne may not have solved 'the Problem of Time' but he did offer a wild surmise of 'powerful . . . emotional vibrancy' [18] to many of a generation desperately grasping for reassuring answers to hard times. Others sought solutions elsewhere — in New Deals, Stalinism, Fascism, psychoanalysis — what is clear is a longing for the ability to hope, a need for guarded or rampant optimism. *A Bride for the Unicorn* is both product and revelation of a major configuration in the personality of its times.

*   *   *

> 'Find me a respectable mythology.'
>
> Leonard the Learned

Matters of time are paramount in *Unicorn,* but Johnston buttresses his themes with subsidiary mythical analogies. He conceived the central theme of the play in terms of myth:

> Myth is the vehicle by which men and women have sought to give expression to their inchoate emotional experience, before the coming of rational understanding. Three thousand years ago . . . astronomy was a closed book . . . so they (our ancestors) invented the story of Persephone and Demeter to understand better the march of the seasons. A little later men pondered over the mystery of the death and burial of the seed and they externalised their wondering thoughts in Christianity. They felt close behind them the presence of the Usurer Death whose book they signed when they accepted the fact of their birth and they turned it into the story of Dr. Faustus.
>
> Today we are nonetheless face to face with the incomprehensible. But it is a new Incomprehensible — the Mystery of Time and the Fear of Death that our every action belies — the Fear of Death so present in our conscious mind but which our subconscious so clearly repudiates in everything we do. For everything we strive after is only to bring it nearer. Here is a paradox that until higher mathematics can explain to us the nature of Time and Space we will never solve intellectually. It is enough to do what the author has tried to do, namely to externalise it in the form of a story the text of which might be "the greatest illusion of all is that we fear the End".[19]

71

Twentieth century literature, seeking ancient structures to house modern instances, seems almost obsessed with myth-making. Much has been written about the death of common values and old certainties in which men found a sense of continuity and tradition; updated myth is a way of recreating a sense of the past, of stirring identification of reader and fictional character, of combatting alienation and reviving heroic possibility. Mythological parallels lend resonance to immediate events, 'meaning and value to a society almost without them', and 'permanence to the impermanent'.[20] Used ironically or as parody, myth can be a painful device to show modern man how inescapably small, unheroic and alone he is; used seriously, myth can generalize and heroicize, relate the individual to the world and reveal him to himself. Often, myth is used both ways in the same work, mixing 'the heroic with the gruesome and hilarious'.[21] *Ulysses* is the obvious triumph in this mythical mode which includes *A Bride for the Unicorn*. Growing used to the fact that Johnston sees at least two sides of every issue, we are not disconcerted by the fact that when he chooses the 'quest' form of myth to 'externalize' his themes, he chooses not one quest but two as structural frameworks for *Unicorn*. The first is a serio-comic treatment of the heroic quest of Jason and the Argonauts for the Golden Fleece, the second the entirely serious and successful quest of the hero, John Foss, for his lost bride.

Though he uses the framework of the Argonaut's voyage in search of the Golden Fleece, Johnston never intends the kind of systematic analogy to a single source that we find in *Ulysses* nor the intricate parallels to an old myth relived in a contemporary context, as in O'Neill's *Mourning Becomes Electra*. Johnston is merely looking for a celebrated quest which would allow him to take his hero on the voyage of life with stops at stations that provide the playwright with opportunities to satirize a number of his favourite targets. Why, then, does Johnston choose the story of the Argonauts if no *necessary* link exists between it and his themes? For two reasons: At this time in the Irish theatre, the rising popularity of films forced Johnston and the Gate directorate to stress the essential differences between theatre and film and to commit themselves to a living theatre that retained an identity separate from film. Johnston writes at the time of the 1935 Gate revival of *Unicorn*: 'The theatre can beat the screen by a firm exploitation of its . . . essential . . . theatricality. Theatricality upon

72

the stage may, perhaps, be recovered by a judicious use of heroic material or a re-valuation of its modern equivalent.' In *Unicorn* Johnston is using a panoramic heroic story played on a revolving stage to obtain maximum theatricality. The Jason legend provides a hero surrounded by heroes. The 'seven doughty companions' of *Unicorn* allow Johnston to construct a complex network of parody, parallel and contrast with John. For example, for pornographic Lewis the Loving, sex is 'a nice little bit of slap and tickle'; for John it is a mystery that gives him a sense of an existence beyond everyday debasement, the ordinary reality Lewis represents. Contrasts with all the 'argonauts', save sympathetic Egbert the Eccentric, set John apart and create a double perspective of value that exactly parallels the two time perspectives of the play. The self-interests of the Companions clash with John's heroic refusal to capitulate to material values. The Companions quickly come to represent a typical cross-section of humanity whereas John, who has had a glimpse of higher things which he quests to recapture (the Gnostic goddess Sophia [the Masked Lady] in giving herself to John grants him the 'gnosis' or revelation of 'the higher world').

John's heroic struggle to make his life meaningful and not succumb to 'tickling commodity' is heightened by the ironic treatment of several of the Companions as heroes. The stages in the voyage of these heroes are types of important areas of human activity: war, law, business, love. Johnston exploits their quest for his satirical ends. Favourite *bêtes noires*, familiar from *The Moon in the Yellow River,* reappear and are belittled by their heroic context. At the same time, the meanness of individual quests of the Companions for money, sex, or power throw the grandeur of John's quest into high relief.

The Argonaut myth, then, provides occasions for a criticism of society and permits Johnston to present his central character as a questing everyman. Jason fits Johnston's conception of John nicely: both are fond of virgins and prey to domestic infelicity; both are journeyers to the sun. Like Jason, John is: 'ordinary man destined to play the hero's part'.[22]

Less flashly in technique but more crucial in Johnston's attempt to build a play that is itself myth and not merely a revamping of old mythology is the story of the otherworldly lost bride from folklore and saga: 'A lady is lost upon her nuptial night. A very

73

common occurrence . . . in folklore and legend. . . . There was Niam of the Golden Hair. . . . And then you may remember Dietrich of Bern, who spent many years seeking for Virginal'.[23] Since the Masked Lady is an emissary from a higher plane of consciousness, Dunne's Time 2, it is unnecessary to pursue her significance further. She represents Dunne's immortality and its implications for life in Time 1. Rather than write a play that deteriorates into frequent abstract lectures on the nature of time, like Priestley's plays *Time and the Conways* (based on Dunne) and *I Have Been Here Before* (based on Ouspensky), Johnston happily prefers to give theory a local habitation and a name.

One final piece of mythical matter remains: the unicorn of the title. The legend of the unicorn, like that of the Lost Bride, is poignant and charming. 'The unicorn,' writes Johnston,

> is at once the most virile of animals and at the same time it is one of the most chaste. Above all else, it is an animal which cannot be captured alive. . . . It can only be captured by the placing of a virgin on the path on which the unicorn canters . . . and the unicorn, seeing the virgin, is so impressed by her charms and beauty that he comes to her very quietly, lies down beside her and places his head on her lap — whereupon the hunters creep up and capture it in nets.[24]

John Foss is Johnston's unicorn. The mythical beast, yoking such contraries as fierceness and docility, chastity and virility, is a perfect symbolic embodiment of the view that personality and experience are comprised of opposites dynamically interacting within the life cycle. Johnston's unicorn is Blakean; it owes something too to Yeats' unicorn in *The Player Queen*, a play which Johnston admires enormously. Yeats's play consist of a number of variations on the theme of the mask, of characters striving against their natural inclinations for their anti-selves. Relevant here is John's transformation from a monastic adolescent to a virile youth within the larger context of his constant battle not to surrender to his Time 1 self, but to reach for his 'true' Time 2 self.

The unicorn's story dovetails neatly with the Lost Bride legend, the Gnostic theology of revelation and the solar quest for eternal light (in the 1933 version of *Unicorn*, John's last name was Phosphorus, 'light-bringer') to form a multi-dimensional mythical

74

fabric to clothe the myth that Johnston means to demonstrate in this play, that 'the fear of death is an illusion'. The myth of immortality that Johnston made of these myths ('*A Bride for the Unicorn* . . . creates a myth by the aid of myths') is purposive; it fulfills Georges Sorel's description of the function of myth: 'Myth must be judged as the means of acting on the present.' [25] Assuring an immortality which is 'not of another world but of this one', *A Bride for the Unicorn* teaches us a way to live now. 'The purpose of life is life itself': Johnston's myth offers not comforting escape but a responsible confrontation with the here and now.

* * *

No exploration of *A Bride for the Unicorn* would be balanced or rigorous without inquiry into the weaknesses that kept Johnston from including it among his collected works. It would be fruitless to attempt to disprove the theory of time or dispute the ethical ideal, hence the following discussion is limited to faults in structure, characterization and style about which there is some chance for objective agreement. These faults fall into two main categories: the characterization of John Foss: and problems in style and structure arising from thematic intent.

The characterization of John Foss. Johnston willingly confesses the errors he made in the creation of a modern everyman whose life story would embody the playwright's theological and ethical thought. Hilton Edwards, the play's original director, pinpoints the unresolved problem in Foss's characterization:

> . . . in the first production this character was played, by the author's directions, as a middle-aged man, and in the second production, by the author's directions, as a young man of an entirely different personality with hardly a change in the script of the spoken words. This may say something for the universal truth of Mr. Foss as an abstraction, but gives him little hope as a living character. To my mind this is a signficant error.[26]

John is too much of an abstract everyman and not enough of an individualized three-dimensional character to carry sufficient conviction in performance. 'It is possible', says Johnston, 'to create

75

an everyman character who is also psychologically individualized. Look at Faust and Peer Gynt.' [27] In terms of psychology, Johnston plans to reconstruct the play to give us a central character with whom we identify more readily and fully, as we already do in a few scenes as they now stand, especially the portrayals of the loneliness and isolation of John's adolescence and the bitterness and regret of his marriage.

Style and structure. When Johnston loses control of Foss's roundness as a character, it is usually as a result of the tremendous pressure of the philosophical themes he is eager to express. The same urgency of idea occasionally causes a breakdown of dramatic dialogue into rhetorical statement or self-conscious poeticizing which clash with the swift movement of the action and the multi-level mythological design. Unfortunately, it is precisely *because* the playwright has 'something to say' that the style fades at times into the kind of turgid rhetoric Johnston had learned to expunge from his earliest work, *Shadowdance*. Regrettably, the following examples do not suffer violence by being quoted out of context:

> Merciless mystery, hear my huge agony! Stay your pitiless hand. . . . You that have gathered all the treasures of the ages, why must you take so mean a thing as I? You that are so infinitely rich, why must you stoop to filch this beggar's load of mortal life?

> What need to cry aloud my fear, to fight for breath? Nothing could rob me of my love but Death, but if my love, herself, be Death, oh terrors, where are you now? . . . Loosen the bonds that link me to the Earth and let me rise, unshackled by mortality.

The rhetorical excesses are an exact measure of the extent to which Johnston, in his urgency to communicate content, fails to dramatize. He overcame this kind of problem in recasting *Shadowdance*; in reworking *Unicorn* he will have to aim at sustaining throughout the sharp-edged, functional language we find now in Scenes II, III, VI, VII, and IX.

There are excesses too in the use of myth. The desire to write an 'all-inclusive chronicle' leads Johnston into a mythological overkill, as though mere reference to a wealth of heroes and their exploits is sufficient to establish John as an every-hero. The likening of John to Robin Hood, Prometheus, Cuchulain, Batu Khan, King Arthur, Orpheus, Apollo, D'Artagnan, Dietrich of Bern, Alexander the Great, Oisin and so on, while it often, in the subtlety of allusion, flatters the well-read reader's vanity, seems an external way of heroicizing John. The Swiss writer on Johnston, Kaspar Spinner, is deceived by the honorific status myth holds in contemporary literature into accepting the farrago of mythical parallel as an index of profoundly integrated complexity. Hilton Edwards, on the other hand, believes the 'structure . . . is cumbersome and overcomplex'. Edwards suggests that the play would have been more successful in the theatre if the mythological design had been simpler. The Argonaut theme, which allows Johnston to alternate the heroic, parodic, and satiric, meshes superbly with the Lost Bride-Unicorn theme, but Johnston cannot refrain from indulging in massive analogy. The excess of myth, like the rhetorical indulgence, points to Johnston's insecurity about the adequate communication of his ideas. In short, Johnston aims at and falls short of what Dame Ellis-Fermor calls one of the rarest achievements in drama, the successful wedding of 'epic spaciousness *and* dramatic concentration'.[28]

Trying in *Unicorn* to widen his boundaries, to explore the dream journey as a repository for human experience and expectations, Johnston dove, by his own admission, into 'choppy waters'.[29] Fault-ridden though the play may be, even in its present imperfect and unfinished state it is a notable effort, and crucial in the development of Johnston's thought. It is concerned with the eternal themes of life; its embodiment of ideas of time (regardless of their logical validity) answers a deep-seated need for reassurance that life has purpose while it is being lived. We may be suspicious of solutions but we cannot deny that the play confronts essential conflicts. Johnston *is* a believer; he does offer hope for a way out of the infinite repetition of evil, hope which depends on individual perception and courage. Johnston's is a moving vision that offers man a choice; at its centre is a belief in human responsibility and dignity, a dynamic humanism that cannot be logically contradicted. Johnston's true subject, in *Unicorn* and all his plays, is man's responsibility to himself and to other men, a responsibility that requires the man who accepts it — the Johnston hero — to rebel against the norms of society's life of quiet desperation, for in these norms evil is perpetuated. No apostle of the virtues of tradition, Johnston begs and warns us to rediscover our humanity and, like Dobelle and John Foss, to begin to live before it is too late.

THE SENSE OF AN ENDING

'Another Irish dramatist who has never quite fulfilled a splendid early promise is Mr. Denis Johnston', concluded G. S. Fraser in a comparison of Johnston to O'Casey.[1] Johnston was frequently to find himself in a position akin to O'Casey's: his early achievement esteemed, his later work ignored or belittled. The brilliance of Johnston's first three plays has eclipsed his later career. With his sense of humour barely hiding his disappointment, he once characterized his fate after that initial burst of fame: 'It is necessary to correct a widespread impression, put about by unscrupulous enemies, that I died of some unspecified disease in the summer of 1933, and have never written anything since.' Those who did continue to follow his development, he said: 'hailed . . . each play [after *The Moon in the Yellow River*] as worse than the last.' [2]

Johnston was far from done in the theatre; he has written seven plays since *A Bride for the Unicorn*. But he was finished as a pioneering and influential playwright. His 'zeal for experiment' [3] had exhausted itself; no play he has written after *Unicorn* has any reverberating implications for new dramatic forms. Early glory did not spoil Johnston's talent — witness later works like *The Golden Cuckoo* and *The Scythe and the Sunset* — but he was through with the kind of *avant-garde* dramaturgy that had excited Dublin and made him the controversial whiteheaded boy of Irish drama in the late twenties and early thirties. *Unicorn* marks the end of the first phase of Johnston's career as a dramatist.

His later work has been equally divided between the Gate and the Abbey, and none of it can be charged with modernist obscurity or philosophical incomprehensibility. Although it includes in *The Scythe and the Sunset* one of the finest history plays in the entire repertory of Irish drama, Johnston's canon after 1933 also contains a play he deems too poor to republish (*Storm Song*). After *Unicorn* his playwriting is marked by irregularity, discontinuity, unevenness and dispersion of energy. A sure command of theatrical device and an unfailing ability to pace the cadences of his prose never leave him, nor do the grace and elegance of his witty style. The lyrical strains interwoven with humour and rhetorical flourish remain prominent. But the formal elements are never again spectacular. Edwards and MacLiammoir, who felt they had nurtured a dramatist with the potential to realize their dream of a non-realistic, internationally-oriented Irish drama, were dismayed at Johnston's defection from the ranks of the *avant-garde*, though they continued to produce his work. Both, it is to be regretted, contributed to the establishment of the sense of some final chasm between an early talent of the highest order and a virtually trivial later output. Complaining about a simplification in his stagecraft, they view *Unicorn* as Johnston's epitaph:

> . . . the failure [of *Unicorn*] to land itself in the public's lap has been a tragical loss not only to Denis but to the Irish theatre. It has discouraged the extension of an imagination that might have led to an entirely new form.[4]

> *A Bride for the Unicorn* has never quite found a port. . . . Just as he is about to conquer the world of imaginative plays, to give the theatre something really new, Denis . . . proceeds to tread the well-worn paths of theatrical realism.[5]

The differences between early and later Johnston are more subtle than a sudden break in theatrical methods. For Johnston is a touchstone figure, and the story of his first period in the theatre is an index to the whole course of Irish drama in the crucial years 1926–1935. Most theatre histories nominate 1926 as the pivotal date in Irish theatre, the year of *The Plough and the Stars* and O'Casey's determination that he could no longer live or work in Ireland. It is tempting to fix on a splashy event as proof that the Irish audiences were hopeless and never would be able to understand or succour their geniuses. But other significant forces of expansion and change were at work and the three years following O'Casey's departure were the Abbey's most adventurous in terms of design and experiment. The real landmarks in the curve of Irish drama during this era are not O'Casey's exile and the rejection of *The Silver Tassie,* but the work of the Drama League, the breakthrough and rapid demise of Yeats's vision in the Abbey,

the formation of the Gate Theatre and the fortunes of Denis
Johnston's early efforts. Yeats was making a doomed, heroic last
stand against Lady Gregory's artistic conservatism and against
the rashers, chips and holy water mentality of the Abbey audience,
shared by many actors whose blind spots were patriotism and
church. To forge a people's theatre that would also be a theatre of
the spirit proved a heartbreaking dream, but Yeats had the courage
to try, and to try a third and fourth time. Yeats never much
understood Johnston's work, but the appearance of *The Old Lady
Says 'No!'* in 1929, was, at the end of the decade, a culmination of
the climate of freedom and formal exploration Yeats had always
tried to build. Aside from Yeats's own work, *The Old Lady* was
the most experimental Irish play of the twenties. Seen from an
historical viewpoint, Johnston's play carries a weight even beyond
its enormous intrinsic merit. It offered Irish drama a measure of
itself and a challenge. It called attention to itself, as if it were
saying: 'This is what is possible in 1929 in Irish drama; are we
to continue in a new direction or run timidly back to the old?'
In the primarily traditional stagecraft of *The Moon in the Yellow
River,* Johnston seemed to answer by taking back the challenge.
And then in the somewhat chaotic daring of *A Bride for the
Unicorn,* Johnston appeared to be taking up the gauntlet more
boldly than before, going on to wilder terrains than anyone could
have foreseen. Two of his three early plays, then, have a place in
a picture larger than themselves, as summaries of accomplishment
of the Irish theatre as a whole, and as mines of technical advance.

But in turning away from radical techniques that others could
learn from, Johnston paralleled an even more total retreat on the
Abbey's part from the flickering moment of substance Yeats had
managed to win for his dream with the productions of *The Emperor
Jones, King Lear* and *Fighting the Waves.* Each of Johnston's plays
after *Unicorn* is an entity unto itself, with no extrinsic role to play
in rerouting the deep and ultimately unbudgeable channel of conservative drama the Irish theatre had so completely dug for itself.
Every new Johnston play must stand or fall on its own qualities,
and there is no exciting new story to tell about how any of them,
or any other Irish plays, made inroads into a stolid, predictable
situation.

By the mid-thirties the Abbey had become a tedious, faction-
ridden political tool. Yeats had been gradually bowing out from

. . . the day's war with every knave and dolt,
Theatre business, management of men.

Men of talent in other fields but who knew nothing about theatre practice, like Frank O'Connor and F. R. Higgins, suddenly found themselves on the Abbey Board, running the theatre. Ernest Blythe, a former Minister for Finance who had no artistic credentials or sensibility, was named a Director in 1935, with de Valera's blessing. By the decade's end, he was Managing Director. The poet Thomas Kinsella tells in an allegorical passage the bitter story of the Abbey's condition as it passed from visionary to comptroller:

A Tragicomical tale: how the Fox . . .
Found a golden instrument one day,
A great complex gold horn, left at his door;
He examined it with little curiosity,
Wanting no gold or music, observed the mouthpiece,
Impossible to play with fox's lips,
And gave it with dull humour to his old enemy
The Weasel — . . .
He took it, hammered on it with a stick
And pranced about in blithe pantomime. . . .[6]

Yeats wrote in 1939, the last year of his life, the final desolate comment on hope, effort and result: 'The theatre has not . . . gone my way or in any way I wanted it to go.'

The Gate continued to operate and grow during the thirties, though it eventually split into two companies (one headed by Lord Longford in which Johnston worked). Several interesting writers, like David Sears and Mary Manning, turned out talented plays for the Gate, but none out of the ordinary in method. Yeats, of course, kept on throughout the decade writing plays in his uncompromising way, even though there was no likelihood they would be put on with any comprehension. By 1933 the Abbey had reached the form it still retains — frequent new managements putting on time-tested Irish classics or new plays skilfully written to old patterns. And Denis Johnston had given up trying to lead the Irish theatre into undiscovered country.

2 : More Rebels and the Blind Goddess

STORM SONG *and* BLIND MAN'S BUFF

The intellect, craftsmanship, and theatricality which characterize
Denis Johnston's early plays are noticeably absent from his fourth
play, *Storm Song* (1934). *Storm Song* is a slick, colourless three-act
play based on the sojourn of Robert J. Flaherty's film company
on the Aran island of Inishmore during the shooting of *Man of
Aran*. Johnston himself would now be happy could he disown the
work. He omitted it from the collected plays and recently has
dismissed it as: ' . . . a sad little attempt at the popular market.
Storm Song turned out to be more of a burp than a song.'[1]

The making of a film in Ireland was an unusual occurrence in
1932, and Dublin closely followed the company's adventures.
Johnston himself spent some time on Aran while the film was
being shot and the characterization of Szilard is essentially a life
drawing, a dramatization of Johnston's first-hand observation of
Flaherty in action — the tension he generated in his environment,
his brooding turbulence and short temper; his absolute faith in his
material and a dedication to the camera that verged on monomania.
The professional attitudes of Gordon King, the film editor in
the play, and his arguments with Szilard are based on a study of
John Goldman, the young editor assigned to Flaherty. In many
other particulars the play dramatizes fact: the impure motives of
a large commercial producer in backing the film; the huge and
careless expenditure of funds; the director's willingness to endanger the lives of the natives for the sake of a desired sequence.
All turn up as timely twists in the plot.

Flaherty towered over his artistic domain; the centre of interest
in *Storm Song* is, therefore, the tyrannical, inspired director. But
Johnston was unable to sustain the focus on Sziland and the
structure disintegrates into three unraveled strands, with a tepid
love interest and a keenly observed social comedy frequently
taking the limelight. While Szilard appears to be the playwright's
main concern, his characterization is a static 'portrait with no
development'.[2] Szilard's only concern is getting a good storm to
film before his money runs out; he is absolutely unconcerned with
human relationships. But his intensity has a potent effect on those
around him.

We see him primarily through the eyes of his co-workers and visitors. Most dramatically viable are the love-hate reactions of Gordon King. Admiring the grand master of the film craft, sometimes grudgingly, sometimes reverently, King has his own idea on the birth of an art form. To him Szilard represents the pioneer whose work must be studied, mastered and superseded by up-to-date technology. King fancies himself a Galahad sent to revive an atrophied movieland. He provokes quarrels with Szilard on questions of camera-work when the real issue is the establishment of his own reputation, disguising his power urge as an attack on Szilard's competency and inhumane egoism which will not hesitate at the sacrifice of human life: 'Your only idea of God is yourself on stilts.' This battle of the generations comprises what little conflict there is in the play. Johnston starts out by stressing the effect of Szilard on King, but the effect rather than its cause soon begins to dominate the action and Szilard is overshadowed as the main character and lost as the centre of interest. This is a pity, for Szilard in action is thrilling; all his bullying and petulance is forgotten in the infectiousness of his total involvement in his art: 'I know what I want and I take it. . . . I'm going to make something that means something . . . it's going to be a picture the like of which nobody has ever seen before.' Unfortunately, Johnston only briefly dramatizes Szilard's life and its culmination. The psychology and history of the man, which belong *in* the play, are relegated to the playwright's textual notes. The revelation of a one-dimensional character, inspiring though he may be, scarcely sustains a three-act play.

. The final scene of the third act reads as if Johnston himself sensed the play's slimness and grew tired of writing it. During the first two acts a measure of substance is lent by the social comedy and by the clashes of Szilard against both the commercial world and the 'faking' techniques of Gordon King. But Szilard is missing from the last scene and with his disappearance what little excitement the play evokes also disappears. The puerile exposition of act three is indicative of Johnston's loss of interest:

Boy.　　　　　　Say, what's going on 'ere Mister? Ain't the picture over yet?

Commissionaire.　Private Show on tonight. This big Cryock Islands picture they've just released.

Boy.	It's in all the papers! "The Last Gesture of a Giant" they calls it.
Commissionaire.	That's right, my lad. That there Mr. Szilard, 'e was drowned at sea making it. It's going to be a big 'it, if you ask me.

With Szilard gone, the sudden last act shift of focus to Gordon King's decision to forsake love for the movies is anticlimactic. Johnston does not even take the pains to dramatize King's turmoil as an inner conflict leading to a responsible choice between two equally powerful alternatives, but makes the choice depend on the unselfish sacrifice of Jal Joyce. Thus the play unaccountably ends with the interest falling on a third character — Jal Joyce — who in relinquishing Gordon condemns herself to the commercial world he escapes. *Storm Song*, thus, begins with the impending final crisis in the life of a great artist, moves to the first crisis in the life of a future artist (who hasn't even the resolve to make his own decisions) and ends with the sacrifice of yet another character. By the last act curtain Szilard has been forgotten.

It should be obvious that none of the conflicts of *Storm Song* — dedicated art vs. Popular Art, love vs. work, the younger generation vs. the older — are themes to which Johnston is passionately committed. He has written other slight plays, but *Storm Song* is the only play in which he makes no effort to confront issues that matter to him. *Storm Song* is most kindly viewed as a forgiveable lapse in Johnston's usual demanding self-discipline.

The play is simply a commercial potboiler, which ironically condemns commercialism. As Hilton Edwards wrote of it: 'In *Storm Song* Denis Johnston is dealing with what for him is too trivial a subject. . . . He was meant to wield a big hammer on a big anvil, and these tools are wrong for cracking nuts.'[3] Johnston at least possessed the self-critical acumen to omit *Storm Song* from the collected plays and to do his utmost to help the play to an early grave by discouraging its performance. The last production was in Melbourne in 1938.

* * *

Despite the trouble it gave him in *Storm Song*, Johnston did not renounce commercial realism. On the contrary, he struggled with the conventional form and conquered it, producing next a tightly-knit courtroom drama which had a very successful run at the Abbey, *Blind Man's Buff* (1936). Johnston's fifth play is a thorough-going rewrite of *The Blind Goddess,* a 1932 play by Ernst Toller. Johnston omitted *Blind Man's Buff* from his collected plays because of complications with the Toller estate, which stipulated that Toller must be credited as co-author, even though the play was in no sense a true collaboration. Quite the reverse. Johnston's account of his negotiations with Toller is amusing:

> I was on a weekend in the south of England with Toller and he asked me to turn his play (*The Blind Goddess*) into an Abbey play; he wanted it turned into an Irish play for some obscure reason. I hadn't read the play closely at the time but I said I would. And when I read it I realized that I didn't like it and I didn't want to do it at all, so I wrote Toller and said: "If I write this play I will make all your heroes villains and the other way around." He replied: "Alright, go ahead." I was stuck and hoped when I finally rewrote it that if only the opening and closing situations were his he would wash his hands of it and say no, but not only did he insist on its being acted but he insisted on his name being first on the bills. I ended up writing it just because I didn't bother to say no to Toller.[4]

Johnston, saddled with a commitment made in a moment of weakness, did his utmost to turn the outline of Toller's plot into a play in which he could deal with the complexities of the law which he knew intimately from more than ten years of daily experience. For Johnston was an eminently qualified barrister* and the son of a distinguished jurist. He practised law in Dublin throughout his first decade in the theatre. In fact, his official name in the theatre was E. W. Tocher, a pseudonym he was forced to adopt in 1928 because of his law practice.† Therefore, unlike the

---

*See *Chronology* for details.

†Johnston jestingly recalled to me the origin of his pseudonym:
> I don't know how to pronounce it, to tell you the truth. When you practice law, if you don't use a pseudonym, even if everybody knows who you are, they think you're not paying attention to your work. And

content of *Storm Song*, the product of a brief period of observation, the issues of *Blind Man's Buff* were of intense personal concern to Johnston. The accurate dramatization of his experience with and reflections upon the legal process give this play the vitality, immediacy and control that were missing from *Storm Song*.

Toller's play is a tendentious social protest against hypocritical middle class morality and bureaucratic corruption, but it is not without a kind of raw power stemming from the intensity of Toller's convictions. At times, however, it is an almost hysterical outcry against the legal system and 'the State' which persecutes the man who dares to live beyond accepted moral codes. In *Blind Man's Buff* Johnston radically modified Toller to turn a didactic protest play into a philosophical whodunit that portrays the spectrum of attitudes and personalities involved in the implementation of justice. Justice itself is viewed by Johnston not as a fear-inspiring instrument of oppression, but as a problematic, imperfect but necessary social regulator which frequently damages the individual caught up in it. Johnston sought to provide a truthful and tough-minded view of the law as he knew it from the inside.

His changes in the original script reflect a persistent effort to tighten Toller's eight staccato, episodic scenes into three suspenseful acts with interlocking events and personalities. In order to create suspenseful crises, Johnston unabashedly resorted to the time-proven machinery of the well-made play. Each act turns on a timely discovery. In the first act, Chavasse's arrest hinges on the revelation of letters kept locked in his desk. In the second act an extra-marital affair and abortion are dramatically revealed at the climax of a trial. In the third act a missing and presumably non-existent poison bottle (with conveniently undisturbed fingerprints) suddenly appears after six months. The ghost of Scribe seems to be guiding Johnston's pen in this play.

> my father said: "You can't be a barrister and be in the paper under your real name." We were doing some Drama League show [*The Father*] and Lennox Robinson came up with the programme draft in his hand and said: "What name do you want to come under?" There was an evangelist carrying on a meeting across the road; his name was out on the board so I said: "Well, put it down here too."

Johnston's professional name remained E. W. Tocher until he dropped his law practice in 1936 to write for the BBC, shortly after the production of *Blind Man's Buff*.

86

But not entirely; for Johnston is not satisfied with a simple courtroom thriller, neatly tied and subsequently unwrapped by happy coincidence. His serious interest is in the nature of justice itself and he alters Toller's plot to illustrate the capriciousness of the law. His changes allow Johnston to dramatize one of his favourite subjects, the pitfalls of the jury system (which he portrayed satirically in 'The Scales of Solomon' scene in *A Bride for the Unicorn*). Son of a Justice of the Free State Supreme Court, Johnston shared his father's severe reservations about the virtues of judgment by a jury of peers. He is not at all certain that the power to decide human destiny is safer in the hands of a prejudiced and ignorant jury than in the hands of an experienced, educated judge. Thus, with plot changes from Toller, Johnston moves into reflections on the limitations of the jury system and into an overall probe of the problems of the law.

Johnston is equally concerned with the psychological interplay between the legal hierarchy and human nature, the individual suffering inevitable in a system made and run by fallible men. While the Dublin legal world provides an engrossing framework, very skilfully manipulated by Johnston for comedy and suspense, the real centre of dramatic interest is in the effect of the law on the relationship between Dr. Frank Chavasse, the accused murderer, and Dr. Anice Hollingshead, his mistress. Though exonerated, both doctors are professionally ruined by the trial. Yet only Anice learns anything from her experience with the impersonal ugliness of human institutions, and the vanity of the men that run them. Chavasse remains the cautious, self-concerned, frightened man he was when he was willing to cover up the facts of his wife's death or when he insisted on an abortion for Anice rather than risk the *status quo* of his marriage and career. But Anice wrests from her embroilment in the ironies of the law a bitter knowledge that leaves her outcast and alone. Seeing Chavasse as the little man he is, she leaves him, an unmelodramatic ending based on hard choice and suffering. Their brush with 'the blind goddess' leaves Chavasse vowing vengeance while Anice becomes a Johnston realist, dissociating herself from the cycle of revenge through a new awareness of the immense grey area of life's complexities that lies between the blacks and whites of Chavasse's selfish world view or the law's certainties — an awareness that makes compassion possible.

Johnston's success in combining his two professions, law and theatre, only whetted his appetite. He wrote again of the law in *Strange Occurrence on Ireland's Eye* (1956), another full-length murder trial play. But the commercial success of *Blind Man's Buff* did satiate Johnston's need to master conventional stagecraft and happily, in his next play, *The Golden Cuckoo*, though he continues to work in a primarily realistic mode, he returns to the problems of expressing his restlessly original mind. *The Golden Cuckoo* too is a play about justice, but in the theatricality of its social and philosophical inquiry it is a work of a different intellectual order from *Storm Song* and *Blind Man's Buff*. Having learned to mould the well-made play to his purposes, Johnston felt free to return to the fascination of what's difficult.

THE GOLDEN CUCKOO

The Golden Cuckoo (Gate Theatre, 1939) originated in a curious letter sent to members of the Irish bar in 1926 by Francis Walter Louis Alphonsus Doheny of County Kilkenny. Johnston relates the charming story of his initial encounter with this unsung Irish rebel:

> *The Golden Cuckoo* is based upon the exploit of an old man called Francis Walter Doheny, who — oppressed as we all sometimes are by a sense of the injustice of life — went out one evening in 1926, and broke all the windows of a Post Office in Kilkenny, calling this gesture the Saint Edward's-Crown-Barker-Parsival-Ironore-Inoco-One-Man-Rebellion. There was a symbolic significance behind each word of this resounding title, and he also made it clear that his action was not inspired by any personal animus towards the Post-mistress. . . . He then surrendered to a local policeman, and was conducted to the local lockup, singing his "Rational Anthem".
>
> From confinement he issued a statement to the Governor-General, the Provost of Trinity College, the Bishop, and the Bar . . . in which he explained the impelling reasons for his surprising gesture. Expecting to go to jail, as other rebels had done before him, he was utterly confounded when a humane

88

and liberal-minded Judge insisted on turning the issue, not upon the injustice of life, but on the matter of Mr. Doheny's sanity — an aspect of the case that had never occurred to him.

Now it seems to me that this whole incident raises problems of some social importance.[1]

Doheny's extraordinary document, entitled 'The Saint-Edward's Crown-Barker-Parsival-Iron-Ore-Inoco-One-Man-Rebellion', presents a detailed description of the event, and provided Johnston with many particulars for his play. To summarize the account Doheny wrote in the third person: On Whit Monday night, May, 24, 1926, Doheny broke the windows of the High Street Post Office in Kilkenny, intending to do more than £5 worth of damage and secure a jury trial. The windows were smashed with 'a Flagstaff bearing his Own Flag (four stripes, each representing a local professional or official malfeasant, with a fifth added, the racing-colours of the County Solicitor).' He chanted his 'Triple Slogan: No Guns! No Blood! No Burnings!' and proceeded to Parliament Street Civic Guard Station singing his 'Rational Anthem (to the tune of "Come Back to Erin") en route.'

At his trial, Doheny sang his 'Rational Anthem' from the dock, cited Calderon's *El Alcalde de Zalamea* as authority for the justification of 'substantial departures from ordinary lawsome courses', and when the Judge summed up the 'wilful' act of civil damage, Doheny added: 'and malicious'. He was sentenced on 22 July, 1926, to three months in a mental institution, from which he issued his matter-of-fact description of Ireland's most fantastic rebellion. Doheny's wondrous deeds and dismal fate lingered in Johnston's mind for thirteen years until he 'commemorated this heart-breaking old man' in a play which, concerned with integrity and self-respect, is a parable of the fate of the visionary.

Two years after *The Golden Cuckoo* was published in 1954, Johnston received a letter from Doheny, who was at the time 'an inmate of Saint Columba's Hospital' in Thomastown, County Kilkenny, requesting a copy of the play. Johnston, who had no idea that Doheny was still alive, let alone in an asylum, was moved to write a tributary reply to explain to the old man how their lives had intersected though Johnston had not known Doheny personally and Doheny had not been aware of Johnston's existence at all:

Ever since I read the document you sent to the Irish Bar almost thirty years ago . . . I have been haunted by the fascinating social and moral issues that it rises [*sic*]. . . . I remember being deeply moved by what seemed to me a grave injustice, and by the very remarkable answer you made by attacking the Post Office. . . . It seemed to me in many ways to parallel the events of 1916. And if it is a praiseworthy act for 800 men to protest violently against the injustice of life . . . why then should not precisely the same tribute be paid to one solitary hero, who is prepared to do it all by himself. I was still more upset and moved to fury by your description of the Judge raising the question of sanity in Court — which seemed to me to be a monstrous alibi on the part of society, which the Judge represented, in order to excuse itself for what it could not explain away.

Doheny, regrettably, never commented on the play or the tribute.

*   *   *

> 'Rebellion is one of the essential
> dimensions of man. . . . We must
> find our values in it.'
> Camus

The Golden Cuckoo is the third of Denis Johnston's four plays on rebellion; nearly half his total output consists of variations upon this favourite theme of contemporary Irish writing. In *The Old Lady Says 'No!'* and *The Moon in the Yellow River* Johnston made the point that rebellion had lost its reason for being and had become a way of life in Ireland, erupting violently precisely at the times when it would cause optimum interference with the true progress of Irish liberty. Later, in *The Scythe and the Sunset* (1958) Johnston made a characteristic effort to divest the Easter, 1916 Rising of the collar of romance that was choking the facts. But Johnston's canvas in *The Golden Cuckoo* seems much smaller. Insurrection on the grand national and historic scale is not his concern in this play, which is about individual civil disobedience — a one-man rising against social injustice. Yet in scaling down the arena of action to the cruel punishment imposed by society upon the man who dares make a defiant gesture to challenge its rigidly established values, the 'little man' who stands up for his rights, Johnston manages to raise questions as intricate as any generated in the three plays dealing with Ireland's more celebrated troubles.

The bold rebel Doheny is 'commemorated' in *The Golden Cuckoo* as Professor Dotheright (pronounced Duthery; read: 'do-the-right' and note a suggestion of 'dithery', scatter-brained) who makes the 'reasonable' demand in a capitalist democracy to be paid for work commissioned and delivered. Dotheright is carefully introduced as the kind of man whose life style is so far outside the social norm that he can safely be dismissed as a crackpot. He is the eccentric outsider, the self-reliant, self-respecting man who threatens society's unquestioned complacent attitudes and pierces the armour of self-deception, inhumanity and isolation to which men condemn themselves. Dotheright is not one of 'society's cranks' but is 'society's conscience'. If he were given a true hearing, the pillars of society would crumble and new beginnings would have to be made (a successful revolution); naturally society cannot sustain such a dangerous character and must, as one character admonishes, 'get rid of him'. Johnston calls the methods by which society operates 'Functionalism', an ossified set of 'principles' which Johnston clearly considers dishonest, immoral and destructive:

> Our generation distrusts the word What? and only really enjoys contemplating How? It is part of the prevailing philosophy of the day — the philosophy of Functionalism. The ultimate criterion for all questions is not What is it? but How does it operate? Functionalists believe that right or wrong is a matter of what comes off. . . . What is true is what works: what is untrue is what fails to work. The most telling thing about Crime is that it doesn't pay. And here comes the depressing corollary: if it does pay it presumably isn't Crime. . . .
>
> In the absence of a moral law — the supreme What? — we tend to concern ourselves only with the question, How will it deliver the goods? And as nothing really delivers the goods, except in a most temporary way, we have been driven to the lamentable conclusion that nothing is really true. Alarm and despondency follow naturally from this. . . .[2]

In *The Golden Cuckoo* Johnston dramatizes his social thought, unfolding a social philosophy which may be called 'anti-Functionalism', a compassionate social realism which probes, as most of Johnston's plays do, behind historical circumstances and fixed conclusions to the 'What' — the many-sided reality or truth of things. For Johnston, morality *is* the act of examining and challenging the simplistic 'How', which is revealed in *The Golden Cuckoo* as a gigantic network of rationalizations of self-interest and power drives. In Doheny's rebellion Johnston found a perfect symbol for his own work which attempts to mobilize the audience to a critical awareness of its ingrained attitudes by exposing the kind of thinking that applauds, for example, the use of the atomic bomb because it 'worked'. To ask 'What' and not join, support or acquiesce to 'How' is the beginning of a tough-minded, realistic redemption of one's humanity, the embarkation on the journey to self-discovery and community that is the ultimate value for Johnston: 'Every man is entitled to a respectable view of himself and what he stands for and it is natural to struggle for it until we get it.'[3]

Dotheright's humanity is intact; he is the 'compleat' anti-Functionalist who throws the complacent How-society into crisis as he struggles to protect his 'respectable view of himself'. Johnston details Dotheright's misadventures as he comes up against increasingly potent Functionalist adversaries in his search for simple justice. The higher the social position, the more ruthlessly unscrupulous Dotheright's opponents become. Chaplain, the newscaster, is easy game as the themes of integrity versus vanity and firm identity versus loss of self are gently introduced. Chaplain has deluded himself into believing he is a public servant when he is but an insignificant tool of the powers that be. Dotheright's method is, in keeping with the man's whole nature, uncompromising; he cuts through to essentials and forces his opponents to see themselves as they are. The horror is that few can survive truth, then pick up the pieces and begin anew, even though more is lost in evading it. To hold onto an image whose price is death-in-life, his antagonists lash out in retaliation against this gadfly who just won't play by the rules of the game. Dotheright's example is intolerable: 'I have found it impossible to meet with dishonesty and injustice and keep a civil tongue in my head — Whenever I meet a snake, I know that I must put my foot on it.'

Lowd, the newspaper editor, is a more formidable representative than Chaplain of society's power and pitilessness in quashing the little man who bothers it. The editor is the antithesis of Dotheright; he inhabits the world of affairs which values the successful man with 'ability to manage other people'. The stage direction at the head of Scene Two indicates Lowd's opportunism and the typical rationalization of the Functionalist, both of which enable him to submerge his humane impulses until the way of the world becomes his way: 'Though he might like the world to be a better place, he is fully conscious that it is not, and he knows how to make the best of that state of affairs. He is, in fact, a crook with a conscience that is just sufficiently vocal to force him to justify everything he does in terms of a code of realistic common-sense.' Dotheright has come seeking only 'a little honesty in their public dealings from Lowd and his paper'. Not getting it, he turns to legal means but Lowd can buy off Dotheright's lawyer: 'I know how to fix [him].' Dotheright doesn't know anybody to 'fix', let alone *how* to 'fix' anybody. His 'constitutional' campaign to win his 'rights' is hopeless and Dotheright is forced to move on from reason to action, to the 'Second Phase', revolution. What is trivial to Lowd is quintessential to Dotheright who has reached the point at which silence would be self-denial and inaction another triumph for the oppressive Functionalist world. His self-respect is in critical danger; 'confronted with an unjust and incomprehensible condition' he is impelled to act, to 'insist that the outrage be brought to an end'. It is not only a matter of principle, but also one of survival: 'In every act of rebellion, the rebel simultaneously experiences a feeling of revulsion at the infringement of his rights and a complete and spontaneous loyalty to certain aspects of himself.'

Dotheright, charged with purpose and a keen sense of the historical significance of his actions, appears at the local Post Office to do enough violent damage to bring his grievance to public attention. 'Something quite drastic' must be done to 'publicly deface the spurious coinage' of a 'democratic' society whose justice is available only to those who 'play the game' that Dotheright calls 'the divine right of 51%': 'there is only one Evil that matters — Injustice. Injustice is the supreme sin — not in those who commit it, but in those who submit to it. For to do so . . . is to admit that Life itself is evil.' Dotheright smashes the Post Office window, launching a one-man rebellion against the injustices of a democracy that is an insidious tyranny of wealth and position hiding behind

93

the clichéd slogans of free enterprise, social welfare, and majority rule:

> Rebellion against . . . Monarchs and Invaders has long been recognized as a respectable thing. But what about the tyranny of Democracy, which . . . can be even more sinister? At a pinch, Monarchs can be assassinated, but who can assassinate — much less identify — the Common Man? Rebellion is of little avail against the Herd. . . . Yet it can hardly be denied that we live, today, in a community that is fundamentally dishonest . . . a society that maintains itself by a mass of regulations that have no basis in social morality at all, but are merely there to enable bad laws to operate. . . .
>
> It is agreed, of course, that laws must be made by somebody. . . . It is, however, not so certain that any greater divine right attaches to them if passed by 51% of a debating society, rather than by a King in Council. Nor does it necessarily follow that Democracy in office is any less dishonest than the Despot . . . the problem of the individual against the State . . . is more acute than ever.[4]

In act three, Mrs. deWatt Tyler, the wife of an American Senator, proves the most insidious of Dotheright's Functionalist enemies as the world marshals its subtle cruelties to crush the marauder. She makes Lowd's economic ruthlessness seem child's play. In order to keep her name out of the papers, Dotheright is sacrificed; to maintain its own 'reasonable' posture, society must 'fix' him. It can't buy him ('The Professor wasn't after money. He was after something far more important.') Therefore it must destroy him. The fidelity he pays to himself must be discredited. Society can only cope with *his* truth by dismissing him as a cuckoo. An appeal is made to the 'humane and sensible . . . [the] very reasonable Judge' to spare the harmless old man and *only* commit him. When Dotheright is told of the favour his former compatriots have procured so considerately, he is unable at first to grasp the enormity of the betrayal. Despite the incisive clarity of his social criticism he has remained like St. Joan, an innocent, unaware of how far society is willing to go to protect itself ('We're only doing the best we can for you. You won't be long in the asylum.') The farcical mode of the play suddenly turns to total seriousness. The horror of his fate is too incomprehensible for Dotheright to impute to human motive; only a Divine sense of humour could jeer the inner vision of truth it has granted him: 'Men and women can forgive each other. But when the Lord himself chooses to mock his servants who is there to forgive Him?' Dotheright is alone in the Functionalist world. His protest has been smothered by a society which absorbs it into its own perspectives. Utterly bereft of a purpose now, Dotheright willingly goes to the madhouse, the only place left where he can be free.

'One of the things that makes me glad that I ever tried to commemorate this heart-breaking old man', writes Johnston,

> is the fact that his memorial, in its last act, suddenly proclaimed its independence, too, and refused to accept the so-called happy ending I originally attempted to impose on it. I had set out to inveigh against the injustice of society, and against the fact that its considerable rewards and punishments are largely alloted on a basis of chance. But if the only remedy of the unlucky Man of Resolution is that of a lunatic, this is far from being a happy ending, however one may treat it.[5]

In the second scene of the last act, Dotheright returns from the asylum no longer a social revolutionary, for he has learned that the question of justice belongs to the 'sane' world of Mrs. Tyler. He can no longer seek external recognition nor expect the world to change: 'Justice? Do you suppose that I care about Justice? Am I a Stockjobber or Bank Official that I should bother my head over the balancing of payments and accounts? I have left all these things behind. . . . Justice is of little importance when you know that you have been right.' Truth and justice are inner states of being; it is unnecessary to prove anything to the world:

> To a free spirit . . . Justice is . . . a minor matter — a virtue in the eyes of tradesmen, and not something for President Doheny to worry about in the proud security of his One-Man-Republic. It is impossible to punish, or even be sorry, for one who does not design to consider himself punished. His victory and independence are matters of belief, and since he believes in them himself, there is no answer but respectful recognition.

95

The Functionalist can readily overlook Dotheright's rebellion — it didn't work:

What may be praiseworthy for a thousand men to do in armed conflict . . . becomes absurd when it is done by one old man with a flagpole. What would happen if everybody did that sort of thing? But this question is just an abili. Everybody has not done it, and we need not pose that query until they do. At present, only Mr. Doheny has done it. And is the measure of the rightness of his action, the number of people who have backed him up? Is it all a question of mathematics? Yes, says the Functionalist, because Mr. Doheny alone is bound to fail. And since he fails, he must be wrong. . . . So Mr. Doheny suffered the most terrible and subtle of all punishments. He did not go to jail. He went to a lunatic asylum.[6]

Yet Dotheright is not a failure; only his single act of rebellion failed to achieve its original goals. He has succeeded by remaining true to himself and not to a system: 'Affirmation [is] implicit in every act of rebellion'; rebellion is an expression of something 'permanent in oneself worth saving'.[7] There are moments when identity can only be preserved by action, though that action may be but a 'gesture' to an uncomprehending world. There are times too when it is more important to fight than to win, as Dotheright's case or the Easter 1916 Rising ('Dotheright's rebellion seemed to me to parallel in many ways the events of 1916') prove.

And in unforseeable ways Dotheright *has* changed the world of the play a bit for the better. 'Awareness . . . develops from every act of rebellion: the sudden, dazzling perception that there is something in man with which to identify.' Dotheright's destiny helps others, Letty and Paddy, and even Lowd, to find something in themselves worth saving. Paddy abandons his cynical stance for pity, his alienation for confrontation with 'the facts' of a complex and 'unfair' world. Through his association with Dotheright, Paddy is able to rediscover the best in himself, to begin to love Letty again and to undertake the arduous and unending task of facing the facts of reality without losing pity, which is 'the only way to answer back' an unpitying Functionalist society. To generate love, community and commitment in a Functionalist universe is 'a

96

miracle', and Dotheright is 'a Saint', a golden cuckoo in a gilded world — 'a very remarkable bird'. Doheny's shrine is Denis Johnston's funniest play, and his tenderest.

THE DREAMING DUST

Oliver Gogarty once characterized the nineteen thirties as 'an age of contraception, tergiversation, and arguments about Swift'.[1] During the years 1931–1940 seven biographies of Swift appeared in England and America. In the Dean's native land (Yeats said that only the Irish imagination can fully appreciate Swift) the Swift renaissance of the thirties primarily affected the imaginative writers. Before the present century, Swift was the only Irishman of letters whose genius had earned international acknowledgement and modern Irish writers look upon his achievements as a heritage to be 'assimilated into the fabric of [their] minds'.[2] In addition, Swift's turbulent life offers infinite possibilities for identification; everyone can find at least a piece of himself in Swift's agony. Five noteworthy literary contributions emerged from this Swiftian revival: the introductory essay to *Wheels and Butterflies* (1934) in which Yeats claims Swift as an emblem of national life and sees in Swift's personal fate an epiphany of Ireland's destiny; Joyce's *Finnegans Wake* (1939), not a work focused on Swift but one 'into which Swift's life is subsumed';[3] and three Swift plays: Yeats's *The Words Upon the Window Pane* (1930–34), Lord Longford's *Yahoo* (1932), and Denis Johnston's seventh play, *The Dreaming Dust* (1940). Yeats's was an Abbey play; the other two were Gate plays.

To the peruser of dramatic catalogues, it sometimes seems that Swift plays proliferate in Ireland as rifely as rhododendrons, the seeds of one begetting the next. Yeats insisted that Swift is a part of the national mythology, a subject that 'haunts' the Irish mind. Johnston's impulse to write a Swift play, accordingly, originated more as a direct response to the plays of Yeats and Lord Longford than as a desire to engage a weighty Irish theme: 'I first became fascinated by the problem of Swift after seeing Lord Longford's play at the Gate Theatre.'[4] His encounter with *Yahoo* began Johnston's passage through Jonathan Swift's dark grove, an involvement that was to last twenty-one years, during which

Johnston produced a radio programme, several versions of a full-length play, a controversial scholarly article, a biography and a TV script. In all of these Johnston propounded a new biographical approach to the celebrated mystery of Swift's life and character, based on the hypothesis that Swift was Stella's half-uncle. After 'several years of exceedingly interesting research', Johnston wrote a Feature Programme on Swift for the BBC in 1938, entitled 'Weep for Polyphemus'. Johnston is a thrifty scholar; he next turned the results of his excavations into the Dean's buried life into *The Dreaming Dust*, which played in Dublin in 1940. In 1941, Johnston read a paper to the Old Dublin Society outlining his speculations about Swift's relationship to Stella. The paper was subsequently published in *The Dublin Historical Record*. 'The reactions', Johnston writes, 'were catastrophic,' for the theory was brand-new and his attitude to previous biographers iconoclastic. Violent criticism nettled him into presenting his novel interpretation with full documentation — he worked intermittently for eighteen years on *In Search of Swift* (1959), a scholarly biography, or, as Johnston jestingly calls it, 'a tome studded with footnotes and terminating with a Bibliography'. In the same year he published the final version of *The Dreaming Dust* in the collected plays.

Johnston's critique of the Swift plays of Yeats and Lord Longford reveals the ambitious goals of *The Dreaming Dust*:

> A great play or a great novel has never been written about Swift and his associates. Those who have attempted to do so either confined their work to a very small aspect of his life or to a particular incident, or they have perverted the known facts in some way in order to make the characters appear credible.[5]

Seeking the comprehensiveness and accuracy he found lacking in *The Words Upon the Window Pane* and *Yahoo*, Johnston wrote a sprawling play with a number of leisurely scenes depicting Swift's London life. The cast numbered twenty-four characters, including such luminaries from Swift's triumphant London years as Steele, Bolingbroke, Addison and Pope. Johnston realized the play was 'handicapped . . . by too many historical characters' [6] and began his customary procedure of extensive rewriting.

The Dreaming Dust, 'after a moderately eventful life in various other shapes and sizes, and under at least one other title evolved from . . . a play about Swift into a play about the search for Swift. . . . The composition of this play (Johnston writes in a preface) has cost me more time and trouble than anything else I have ever written, thanks to the peculiarity of the material.' In the second of the play's shapes, the 1954 text, Johnston has tightened the 'scattered' structure by condensing the 'episodic picture of Swift in London',[7] eliminating characters, doubling and trebling roles and by focusing more steadily on the psychological motivations of the main personalities. The original version was a product of Johnston's tremendous excitement about his biographical hypothesis; in time the novel content grew familiar to him and he became absorbed in the dramaturgic possibilities of his material. By 1954, he conceived *The Dreaming Dust* as an actor's play, 'an exercise for actors and actresses with a flair for character'. Nor did he overlook any potential for technical innovation:

I have taken an opportunity of constructing [the play] in an unusual way. . . . What is wanted today is a type of play with a small cast of star parts, that can be toured with ease, carrying only props, and maybe some additional lighting equipment, and that can be performed in places where there is not a regular theatre at all — a play that can be staged with an elaboration or a simplification that depends only on the taste and resources of the Manager — from a Cathedral interior with organ and choir to a broadcast with no scenery at all. This is an attempt to construct such a play. . . . Its ideal presentation . . . would probably be . . . as an Interlude in St. Patrick's Cathedral.[8]

Despite Johnston's labours, the inherent fascination of the material, and the optimum production Hilton Edwards finally achieved (in the 1959 Dublin International Theatre Festival), *The Dreaming Dust* has never been a literary or popular success.

* * *

The enigma of Swift's life ranks as one of the supreme attractions for literary detectives. Johnston's imaginative — some say fanciful — contribution to Swiftiana was originally intended as a corrective to the 'confined' stage portraits of Yeats and Lord Longford. Yeats, Johnston contends, presents 'Swift [as] a man haunted by the fear

99

of madness and unwilling to marry on that account. Yet there is nothing in Swift's works or correspondence to suggest any fear of insanity, least of all a fear that would prevent his marrying.' In *Yahoo*, Lord Longford

> alters most of the essential dates [and] presents the conventional picture of the two women popularised by the great Victorian writers — Stella as the trusting, humble little *ingénue* doing whatever she is told, even to the extent of deep self-humiliation — Vanessa as a forward hussy pursuing the Dean with her unwelcome attentions. Yet a study of their lives and correspondence reveals that neither of these women was the slightest like that.[9]

The ingenious biography Johnston unfolds in *The Dreaming Dust* originates in the dramatist's need to reconcile fact and behaviour, to reconstruct credible motivation for *all* the characters who moved 'within the gravitational field of Dr. Swift':

> It would be comparatively easy to draw a stage portrait of the Dean of St. Patrick's as a scatological problem-child with a hatred of the sex act and an obsession with lavatories, or as a tormentor of women who drove two of them into the grave, or simply as an unusually angry old man.
>
> Unfortunately the matter does not end here, as there are other characters to be considered as well as Swift, and if we stick honestly to the data in the case of these also, we find ourselves struggling in a Bedlam of eccentrics. . . .
>
> A character in a play has to be explained sooner or later to the player who is expected to portray it, and this is no easy task if his or her behaviour bears no resemblance to any known pattern of human conduct, or even to some convention of the stage. Yet here we have a set of characters actually taken from life, the oddness of whose conduct is inescapable, whatever their real motives may have been . . . a speculative story invented to account for the peculiar behaviour of a given set of stage characters may perhaps turn out to be closer to the truth than was at first supposed.[10]

Any biography of Swift that seeks to understand the behaviour of the three central characters must answer the key question:

Were Swift and Stella married? Both a negative and a positive answer generate a series of secondary puzzles. If they were married, Johnston queries, why was it kept a secret? Why would Swift take scrupulous care never to be seen with Stella except in the presence of a third party? Was Stella the masochistic 'half-wit' she would have to have been to endure such a situation while Dublin buzzed with gossip of the Dean and Vanessa? Or the corollary: Was Swift a sadistic misogynist, an adulterer who revelled in his wife's and mistresses' torments? If they were not married, why did Stella never marry? Why did she for twenty years 'accept not only [Swift's] protection but also his money'? Why didn't Swift marry Vanessa, or anyone else? Why did he suddenly sever his relations with Vanessa in the spring of 1723 (to which she reacted by falling into an anxiety-ridden depression that hastened her early death from consumption)? Any answer confronts us with a Gothic tale of cruelty, spite, self-effacing martyrdom and hysteria unless a plausible chain of events can be reconstructed that would return the principals from the far reaches of neurotic activity to within the bounds of reason. Johnston hypothesizes an answer which he claims would enable us to see the trio as rational beings behaving as intelligently as possible in a bizarre situation.

Johnston's solution (presented in detail in *In Search of Swift* and dramatized in *The Dreaming Dust*) is that Swift and Stella could not marry because their union would have been incestuous. He concludes that there was truth in the belief popular during her lifetime that Stella was the illegitimate daughter of Swift's patron, Sir William Temple. Swift, as he emerges from Johnston's search, is Sir William Temple's half-brother and Stella's half-uncle. Though a number of suppositions are required to reach this solution, the answer *does* explain facts otherwise difficult to account for, such as: Sir William's employment of Swift as his secretary-protegé; the financing of Swift's Trinity and Oxford education, supposedly paid for by his uncle Godwin Swift who could not afford to educate his own sons; and the claim of Swift's mother to be well-connected with the Temples. Above all, it provides a consanguineous link between Swift and Stella. Their marriage, Johnston shows, would have exposed them to a possible criminal charge of incest for it would have violated a secular law of the early eighteenth century.

Yeats wrote that 'Swift is always just around the next corner...there is no satisfactory solution' [11] to the Swift mystery. Johnston's central point is that his theory, though it cannot be definitely proved cannot be definitely disproved either, and that 'once one accepts it everything else falls neatly into place. . . . It is the only explanation that I can find which motivates the behaviour of the characters. To that extent, I believe as a Dramatist that it must be true.' [12]

Granted a 'solution to the Swift tangle' which 'could be the true one', Johnston is still faced with the questions of why Stella never married and why, if she was but a beloved relation under his protection, Swift did not marry the importunate Vanessa. To deal with these conundrums, Johnston shifts from the investigation of external events to psychological suppositions. He concludes that Stella was aware of her own bastardy but not her tutor's, and fell deeply in love with Swift. Informed of the facts by Swift, she was nonetheless eager to commit herself to a future as his companion rather than marry some pedestrian suitor. Swift was profoundly flattered but overestimated his self-control, imagining that Stella's intellectual love would sustain him. So it did, until he had to cope with the frank sexuality of Vanessa. He yielded and for a time dwelt in a captain's paradise — a woman in Ireland for the mind and one in England for the body. But in 1723 Vanessa had the poor taste to come to Ireland to pressure Swift into marrying her or confessing his marriage to Stella, thereby forcing Swift into an unwelcome resolution of his mind-body problem. At this critical juncture in his fortunes, Johnston's Swift is tragic, trapped by alternatives either of which must destroy a woman he loves: to choose is to suffer and cause suffering. This Swift is no moral 'monster' or psychosexual infant: Johnston's Swift is nothing but a man, caught between passion and allegiance, appetite and honour, tormented and immobilized by pity. The tragedy is underscored by the irony of his birth, an instance of what H. L. Mencken calls the 'harsh fiats of destiny'. Swift is incarcerated in an emotional prison not completely of his own making, a victim both of circumstances and self-deception. Swift's decision in the climactic scene of *The Dreaming Dust* is a response to Stella's pride, the primary trait on which Johnston builds her character. She grants Swift freedom to marry Vanessa, but only on the condition that he expose the true nature of their relationship, so the world will not ridicule her as a 'cast mistress'. Swift elects to honour his mother and protect Stella's reputation. Vanessa, a woman scorned, unleashes her more than hellish fury by appointing George Berkeley to succeed the Dean as her executor (which resulted in the publication of the revealing 'Cadenus and Vanessa') and by dying within a month, paying a rather high price to guarantee the Dean's perpetual guilt. Stella remains tranquilly devoted to Swift until her death five years later.

This new biographical interpretation which Johnston unfolds has been judged 'the most comprehensive and convincing explanation of Swift's life',[13] and 'a thesis [that] certainly explains a great many otherwise unexplained evasions, lies and animosities'.[14] Johnston's most passionate advocate has been the irrepressible Gogarty, who commented in his best Buck Mulligan manner: 'All [Swift's] biographers leave us with is . . . an enigma. There is but one exception . . . Denis Johnson [sic]. To him the solution of the jigsaw puzzle is due. His findings have been accepted by me.'[15] On the other hand, any theory that challenges the methods and conclusions of previous work is bound to be defensively reviled, as Johnston's has been by such biographers as Evelyn Hardy and Middleton Murry.* Not likely to be the last word on Swift, Johnston's solution will nonetheless have to be reckoned with by any future investigator.

* * *

*While my purpose is not to defend or repudiate Johnston's hypothesis, the interested reader may want further bibliographical guidance. The distinguished Swiftian scholar, Sir Harold Williams, challenges Johnston on the basis of the deeply respectful tone of Swift's remarks upon his mother's character soon after her death (*Times Literary Supplement,* 29 November, 1941, p. 596). Sir Harold's refutation typifies the reaction of academic Swiftians, among whom Johnston's theory has no currency whatever. Yet it ought to be pointed out that Sir Harold offers contrary evidence but does not challenge the validity of Johnston's evidence, only the overall conclusion. Herbert Davis uses the same argument in *Jonathan Swift* (New York: Galaxy Books, 1964). Neither confronts the basic assumptions on which Johnston bases his argument: the data of the death of Jonathan Swift, Sr., or the paternity of Stella, which are especially vulnerable. The *Times Literary Supplement* itself, on the other hand, devoted its lead editorial to the theory in its 13 September, 1941, issue (p. 459) and accepted it for its daring and comprehensiveness. In all fairness it ought to be noted that these grounds are no more logical, when applied specifically to Johnston's case, than those of the other side.

103

It took Denis Johnston nineteen years to cast these absorbing, complicated biographical speculations into a play that satisfied him. The biographical theory remains constant throughout the metamorphoses of *The Dreaming Dust*; therefore in changing the structure Johnston was either seeking more theatrically effective ways to tell Swift's story (merely elaborating the same content into an increasingly more involved form) or he was reflecting some kind of growth in his conception of the subject. Hilton Edwards has asserted that *The Dreaming Dust* is, in that damning book reviewer's phrase, 'merely a fictional biography'. Edwards charges that the work is a 'thesis' play masquerading in fancy dress: 'Denis in *The Dreaming Dust* . . . combines with his newly acquired realism something of the theatrical freedom of the technique of his first two plays . . . but the whole work sacrifices drama to a thesis.' [16] By Johnston's admission, the version Edwards produced in 1940 was 'straight biography', but he claims to have changed this theatrical detective story into a 'tragedy' of thematic import beyond 'the personal problems of Swift'. The major question the play raises is whether Johnston has succeeded in making a play about Swift into a Denis Johnston play. Does *The Dreaming Dust* reflect the serious themes of this philosophical playwright, or is it, like *Storm Song*, a curio atypical of his canon?

All three versions open in St. Patrick's above the graves of Swift and Stella. In the earliest version (1940) the form is a simple play-within-a-play in which the 'dust' of Swift and Stella 'dreams' its history by 'possessing' the bodies of the several visitors to their tombs. The choice of a dream framework allows Johnston considerable freedom to roam through history non-chronologically in order to portray Swift at several critical moments in his life. Chronological time sequence is violated; the events are ordered psychologically. Johnston takes known facts and asks: 'What must have happened to account for this behaviour?' But aside from a 'brave show of novelty' in 'the manner of its construction', the form of the '40 version is wholly subservient to Johnston's thesis. The second version (1954) is significantly different from the first. The time is 1835, date of an exhumation of the bones of Swift and Stella. The characters gathered at the graves are now actors who are asked by the current Dean to be 'advocates for each of the Deadly Sins'. They proceed to enact a half-seance, half-dream play in which they become the manifestations of the uneasy spirits of the principal historical characters. The main weakness of this middle text is the unexplained presence of the actors in the church. The arbitrary appearance of actors who happen to be well-versed in Swiftiana and who in a matter of moments launch into a full-fledged biographical drama puzzles the audience and works against the suspension of disbelief. It stirs at the outset an impression of contrivance and creates audience skepticism which the rest of the play must struggle against.

The final version (1959) corrects this self-defeating structural impediment. The actors now have just completed a 'Masque of the Seven Deadly Sins' in the Cathedral. Two women are returning the skulls of Swift and Stella after they have been circulated among a group of phrenologists convened in Dublin. The women precipitate an argument among the masquers who each take positions representing the conflicting popular myths surrounding Swift's life and character. As in the middle version, the Dean then suggests that they let Stella and Swift dream their stories aloud. From this point on, with the exception of minor stylistic improvements, the '54 and '59 versions are identical. The movement of both versions resolves after the prologue into an ingenious variation on the courtroom drama we meet repeatedly in ex-barrister Johnston's plays. Each of the seven 'sins' attempts to unravel Swift's mystery by accusing the Dean of a particular sin and arguing a case which attempts to disprove the testimony of the previous deadly sin. In this manner Johnston collates the traditional views of Swift and exposes not only the inadequacy of their one-sidedness but also the motives for each biased interpretation. Bishop Berkeley, for example, the butt of Swift's uncanny insight into hypocrisy and opportunism, revealingly defends himself by charging Swift with being 'jealous of everyone who was more successful than himself'. From this attitude stems the belief that Swift became 'a hater of the human race' because of the disappointment of his hopes for political and ecclesiastical advancement, a point of view which entirely omits any circumstances of Swift's private life as a possible cause of the bitterness of the last twenty years of his life. Thus, Johnston simultaneously criticizes views of Swift based on ab-stracted, isolated segments of the Dean's life and welds each piece of discredited evidence into a link in the chain of his own argument. The seemingly episodic scenes are actually arranged according to a calculated courtroom logic leading to the climactic revelation of Johnston's case, which is finally presented as the only one that can fulfill the masquers' requirements for comprehensible motivation.

Johnston, however, did not introduce the seven deadly sins solely as an organizing framework for his biographical argument nor simply for increased histrionic flamboyance. On the contrary — it is precisely this addition that embodies the thematic possibilities Johnston gradually discovered as he pondered the details of Swift's life for over fifteen years: 'Theatrically it [*The Dreaming Dust*] has long since ceased to be as much concerned with the personal problems of Swift as with the seven deadly sins, their relative deadliness, and the curious phenomenon that it is usually our own particular sin that we find really unbearable in other people.' [17] *The Dreaming Dust* is a chronicle of seven attempts to comprehend a man by finding ourselves in him: 'I suppose it is our faults that we have each accused [Swift] of. Perhaps that is the only sin that any of us can understand and the only one that nobody can forgive.' Johnston does not wish to exonerate Swift from the charges; what he challenges is the eagerness of Swift's contemporaries and succeeding generations to accuse and judge myopically, each era forcing Swift into its own field of vision. Swift, Johnston holds, is not innocent but guilty of *all* seven sins. All men are; it is the human condition according to Johnston's theology. Man is 'born with his sins'; they are 'inheritances . . . legacies'. The sins, or evil, are part of the divine scheme and man's greatness resides in his sins as well as his virtues, for the Lord is the Creator of both 'Good and Evil . . . the frost and the flowers'. The exhilirating tragic emotion, the gaiety transfiguring all the dread of Johnston's Swift, is the masquers' (i.e., the audience's and hopefully posterity's) relinquishment of the easy reaction of self-protective condemnation for the more difficult choices of pity and forgiveness for this 'colossal', suffering sinner. Johnston wants Swift's tragedy to create in its beholder the power not only to accept but to *rejoice* in tribulation as 'part of the fabric of life itself'.[18] Johnston's purpose in *The Dreaming Dust* is to teach us the wisdom he wrested from his own spiritual turmoil during World War II. In the 'Paradiso' ending of *Nine Rivers to Jordan* (published in the same year that *The Dreaming Dust* appeared with the added seven sins theme) the Acolyte (Johnston's *persona*) learns from the Voice of the Lord that the splendour of life lies as much in the violent struggle wrought by evil as in love. Grace, man's partaking of the divine will, is joyous reconcilement to evil, the recognition of the wonder in human woe. Johnston's Swift knew both love and suffering in abundance. He is a magnificent sinner, great in the magnitude of his aliveness, a vitality which encompasses the seven deadly sins. 'His sins need no punishment from us, whatever [they] may be.'

Johnston's legacy to us, the comfort of Swift's tragedy, is that we are not impotent in the face of evil and suffering, immobilized by 'tempests of malediction' in the eyes of which we rage against our god. We have alternatives to 'the holy anger of sinners confronted by sin' [19] — pity and the power of acceptance. Swift, himself a pitying man who could not be cruel to Vanessa when 'cruelty was the only thing that could have saved her', has been damned and posthumously psychoanalyzed but not simply pitied. The labours of Johnston's research were devoted to a formation of the facts of Swift's life that would redeem him from obloquy and permit us to know Swift not as a legend or case history but as a soul in torment. In the only play which he calls a tragedy, Johnston's portrait asks us to pity Swift in the sense in which Joyce defines tragic pity: 'Pity is the feeling which arrests the mind in the presence of whatsoever is grave and constant in human suffering and unites it with the human sufferer.'

In the final analysis, Johnston has succeeded in uniting biographical material and personal vision. Perhaps there is the stuff of great tragedy in Swift's bitter story. If so, it is not realized in this play or any other. Yet *The Dreaming Dust*, with its novel form, elegant prose style and excellent acting roles, is the most stageworthy version of Swift's life that has come out of the Irish theatre.

A FOURTH FOR BRIDGE *and*
STRANGE OCCURRENCE ON IRELAND'S EYE

The Dreaming Dust in 1940 marked the end of Denis Johnston's persistent loyalty to the craft of playwrighting. In the twelve years between 1929 and 1940, he produced seven plays and was the most prominent young Irish dramatist of his generation. But by the late thirties his interests began to change. He had already joined BBC Radio in 1936 as a script writer and soon after turned to television.

During World War II, Johnston distinguished himself as a correspondent in Africa and Europe. He re-created his war experiences in the memorable and highly original *Nine Rivers from Jordan* (1954). After the war, Johnston embarked on a successful academic career in American universities.

During the last thirty years Johnston has written only three plays: two for the Abbey and a one-act play which has been done on television. In the past dozen years he has written nothing at all for the theatre. Consequently, his reputation has suffered from the sporadic nature of his output and he has become one of those dramatists — like Hauptmann and Maeterlinck — who long outlives his period of intense creativity and celebrity. Johnston has ceased to be a living force in Irish drama, and his work has nostalgic rather than immediate associations.

Johnston's work as a dramatist falls into three distinct blocs or phases: 1929–1933, the period in which, as a daring experimentalist, he incorporated the most advanced European modes into a personal, very Irish voice; 1934–1940, a period marked by regular productions which were eclectic in form and widely varied in subject matter; and 1948–1958, a phase which contains a brilliant one-act farce and a play about the Easter 1916 rising which deserves to survive among the best plays of the Irish theatre. This later period reveals undiminished his genius for irony, lyricism, theatricality and intellectual depth. It begins with the war comedy, *A Fourth for Bridge,* Johnston's only one-act play.

* * *

In *A Fourth for Bridge* (1948), Denis Johnston continues his campaign in the theatre for the de-mythologizing of history and social institutions. Previously, Robert Emmet, the Troubles, Irish jurisprudence, capitalism and the life of Swift had undergone the scrutiny of Johnston's ironic eye; in this play he anatomizes the propagandistic party lines of World War II. Johnston asserts that *A Fourth for Bridge* was intended 'to spoil the official myth' that World War II was a 'struggle between villains and heroes'.[1] Time, Johnston maintains, frequently overshadows the initial clearcut issues of war. For example, present perpectives indicate that the war was 'actually . . . a row between the United States and Russia'. Since with time issues blur and allies become enemies, Johnston suggests that in war 'behaviour is much more important than the issues',[2] at least for the dramatist. Behind the madness of death camps, saturation bombing and thermonuclear attack are the individual fighting men — indoctrinated with national shibboleths, but essentially sane while surrounded by war's absurdities, and sharing the same human concerns, whatever side they happen to be on. For Johnston, the significance of war is to be found in its effect on the men who fight it — a matter of personal experience, not grand causes or epochal battles.

Though Johnston labels this little play 'a squib' and *a morceau* his prefaces belie these flippant appraisals. He intends to accomplish no less than the setting straight of the record — the correction of the melodramatic ways in which World War II had been presented on the stage:

> There have already been a number of plays that describe very accurately the physical circumstances of that extraordinary war, but none, that I can think of, that reflect its spiritual confusion, and the amusing chasm between theory and practice that confronted most of the fighting men.
>
> Looking back on it now . . . it appears to me to have been a superb example of the fact that War as a phenomenon can no longer be regarded melodramatically. . . . It is a social disease; . . . it is time we stopped talking about it as a Crusade, and looked at it from the clinical point of view of half a dozen friendly enemies trapped in an aeroplane. It will not be the official attitude, but it will certainly be a realistic one.[3]

To dramatize the realistic, human side of war Johnston appropriated a delightful 'true story' for the basic situation of *A Fourth for Bridge*. He recounts the incident in *Nine Rivers from Jordan*. This real event reads as if it were a summary of the kind of 'absurd' or 'black humour' war comedy popular today:

> Two RAF men . . . had been captured by the Italians and taken for internment to the island of Pantellaria. Having arrived there with their escort, it was discovered that there was nobody available on Calypso's island to make a fourth at bridge, so the party set out again by air for Sicily, in search of another player. It was a very bumpy day, and before

long the escort began to feel airsick. When he was no longer interested in anything except the condition of his stomach, the prisoners gently relieved him of his gun, and went forward to talk to the pilot. To him they broached the fact that they now wished to be brought to Malta . . . but the pilot said, No. He was due for some leave and would obviously lose this if he went to Malta. A long argument followed, in the course of which the very peculiar situation was discussed. The Britishers pointed out that as they had a gun and were in a position to shoot the pilot, they ought to be regarded as in control of the plane. The pilot . . . argued with equal force that if they shot him, the plane would crash — unless they knew how to fly it themselves — a matter on which he could hardly be expected to give them instruction. . . .

Before the petrol ran out, a compromise had to be reached. So by agreement the destination was changed to Malta, on the understanding that the aircraft . . . would ever afterwards be confined to the neutral and humanitarian task of spotting airmen of both sides who were unlucky enough to fall in the drink. . . . And there the plane is in Malta to this day. . . .

How significant it is that such tales are poison to the authorities on both sides. No breath of anything of the kind is ever allowed to pass the censors.[4]

Johnston transforms this anecdote into 'a characteristic mixture of fun, irony and gravity.'[5] Inside a rickety Italian aircraft Johnston packs a sharply caricatured international motley of strange bedfellows reminiscent of the *dramatis personae* in such absurdist war comedies of the nineteen sixties as *Catch-22* or *Dr. Strangelove*. At first, we seem to be watching an entertaining little farce which exploits every comic opportunity of its situation. For example:

German.   There is no smoking on this airplane.
Hussar   (*lighting up*). You don't say.
German.   It is an Italian airplane. There is always danger that it blow up.

But the issue soon becomes survival, and the protective masks of national identity are dropped. Hard nationalist lines crumble and the uproarious exchanges of insult and cliché shade into an atmos-

110

phere of community. The passengers, who comprise a microcosm of the European war theatre, are war-weary, exhausted from the tension of maintaining patriotic pretense. They enact a symbolic disarmament which is followed by a mutual unburdening of the load of transparent lies they have been conditioned to tell themselves. Freed of playing roles imposed by history, the occupants of the plane enter wholeheartedly into a brief interlude of joyous apostasy that momentarily brings them close to each other: 'I am bored with Poland. . . . Mussolini makes me sick. . . . You can throw in our far-flung Empire — the father it's flung the better. . . . Hitler is a crazy lunatic.' They crown this abandon by violating the no-smoking rule together — a symbolic peacepipe ceremony and communion. The permanent human bonds underlying temporary political isolation reassert themselves long enough to separate the real from the histrionic. When the plane lands, they have to play the game again, to go, as one character sardonically remarks, 'back to reality' — to the impersonal war which inescapably surrounds any individual breakthrough to the personal. But what is valuable, the core of shared humanity, has been unmistakably established.

While on one level this brisk farce is designed to accomplish Johnston's avowed purpose of substituting realism for romance, on another it is a very personal play, a record of the playwright's reactions to his own war experiences. *A Fourth for Bridge* may be viewed as a companion piece to *Nine Rivers from Jordan*, a theatrical counterpart to autobiography in which Johnston chronicles his own 'spiritual confusion' and struggle to comprehend the place of this war, initially to him an image of Absolute Evil, in a divinely ordered scheme. The absurd violence of the war offered an imminent threat to accepting reconciliation with the evil that had been the core of Johnston's theological resolution. The play is a parable of the complex of event, thought, and feeling that enabled him ultimately to integrate even the war into his philosophy. Moving daily among the fighting men, Johnston noticed

> that quite a number of people . . . had a much better time during the last war than they had ever before or since. That peculiar upheaval was a human disaster of the first magnitude, and the most widespread experiment in ruthlessness that the world has yet experienced. Yet on many occasions it evoked a most peculiar friendliness between the men who were en-

111

gaged in killing each other, and a feeling of warmth . . . that was totally out of keeping with what was portentously called the "War Effort".

Johnston came to see the war pragmatically, or as he playfully puts it, in a 'heretical and antisocial' way:

> Man has always known that war — in reasonable quantity — is good for the metabolism, and on the few occasions on which the Almighty has . . . given peace in our time for unreasonably long periods, we have had to invent a war. . . . So if scientific developments are now going to force peace on us as a permanency, it is a poor lookout for our descendants. They will have a right to be even more angry than they are, if they cannot have a decent fight now and then without blowing all civilization to smithereens.[6]

In addition to this 'subversive to the point of blasphemy' view that war is a cathartic safety valve for aggressiveness, Johnston reaches the empirical conclusions that, purposeful or not, war is a fact of nature ('war appears to be inevitable in this life') and that violence is a movement in the natural rhythm of existence.

Ultimately, Johnston finds in war the 'virtue of violence', the exhilaration of conflict. We meet this notion repeatedly as a central value in his plays. The fear men live under in wartime 'can serve to heighten the perception and to quicken the emotions. It is a bond that can link men together in a brotherhood that will outlast all other bonds.'[7] Thus, despite its partisan issues, war, as this 'humouresque in an airplane'[8] illustrates, cannot crush man's dignity and basic impulse to connect with his fellow man. The play is a testament to the 'sanity of behaviour'; a glimpse behind the public face of war ('the official myth') reminds us that 'men on the whole are sane'. And, Johnston adds, 'it is a good thing to be able to say so', to find even in war confirmation of his 'cheerfully realistic view of Man'. Though *A Fourth for Bridge* may bear a superficial resemblance to the comedy now associated with the school of 'black humour', it is his optimistic faith that even in the midst of death there is life — an essential belief in the intelligence and moral nature of man — which dissociates Johnston from the radical doubt and gallows humour of the absurdists.

* * *

Ever frugal with the products of his imagination, Johnston next rescued a shelved radio play of 1936 and expanded it into *Strange Occurrence on Ireland's Eye* (1956), a courtroom drama which brought him back to the Abbey after a hiatus of eighteen years. *Strange Occurrence* is *Blind Man's Buff* all over again (even down to the detail that both were box-office hits at the Abbey), except Johnston was now able to publish his 'sober reflections on [his] earliest and best-loved profession' in the collected plays under his own name. Johnston wanted to make a permanent dramatic statement of his thoughts on law, justice and truth to stand independent of a 'supposed collaboration' with Toller. He assures the reader that 'the crime and characters are entirely different'. But differences are superficial: many lines are repeated from the earlier play; the defendant is convicted by the same idiosyncrasy in the law of evidence; the case is reopened by a similar string of coincidental discoveries. Theme as well as plot is repeated in *Strange Occurrence,* for both plays comment on the gap between an ideal of justice and a pragmatic legal system. The only notable difference from *Blind Man's Buff* is the replacement of emphasis on the psychological effects of the miscarriage of justice by a new interest in the *process* by which justice can malfunction.

The plan of the later play is exceedingly simple. The first two acts delineate the process by which the legal system functions as 'part of a ritual of public revenge'. A death in unusual circumstances comes under suspicion; there is an exhumation, then the discovery of a motive and several bits of circumstantial evidence which lead to a trial and conviction. The defendant is William Burke Kirwan, a bohemian artist whose sexual misconduct makes him, in the public eye, capable of any crime. Kirwan, 'a scandal to a Christian country', is the victim of 'hysteria and stupidity', condemned by a society which cannot tolerate eccentricity. The third act is primarily a late nineteenth century style discussion of preceding events.

This last act focuses on the dichotomy between the ideal and the actual in the operation of legal institutions. 'Common sense' and 'long experience' convince the police that a character as 'morally obnoxious' as Kirwan 'was clearly guilty of something or other . . . whatever he is, he's not innocent. It it's not one crime it's another.' Johnston makes this point wittily in the preface: 'One can see Mary Magdalene being triumphantly committed for contempt of court, had she shown any natural reluctance to answer the question, "Are you prepared to state that you are not, and never have been, a whore"? Law, then, is distinct from justice, and functions as a socially expedient instrument for weeding out undesirables. As the senior counsel for the prosecution remarks: 'It's law — not justice. There's a subtle distinction. Justice is something that is properly reserved for the Deity. We're not so presumptuous as to aspire to that. All we can do is to play a game called law, according to certain rules, and hope for the best.' Kirwan's ex-mistress bitterly assaults this professional attitude:

> People are only black or white to you. A man is an unattractive type — so he can be hanged for something he didn't do. . . . With people like you it doesn't seem to be a matter of finding out the truth. To you this whole business of a criminal trial is just a game — a game that has nothing to do with guilt or innocence. It all depends on who has the best set of tricks. Bill Kirwan hasn't been convicted because he's guilty, but because he didn't play the rules as smartly as you people did.

But Johnston has no desire to portray the men who implement the law as deliberately vindictive villains, amassing convictions to allay politicians' fears in the face of public unrest ('the truth [is] a dangerous luxury for a public servant to get addicted to') or to secure their own jobs. The professionals 'burdened with the enforcement of law' begin to trust the lessons of experience which convince them of a man's guilt and lead them to push hard for a conviction in cases where evidence is skimpy and circumstantial:

> . . . the criminal courts on both sides of the Atlantic do not often break down at the expense of the individual, and whenever they do, the cause of the trouble is not usually malice, corruption, or any active ill-will on the part of the State. It is much more likely to be brought about by what may be described as the common-sense short cut, and the professionalism that springs not from hard-heartedness, but from long experience.

In most of Johnston's plays, a central character is placed in a high stress situation that results in a radically new awareness of reality. In this play, Brownrigg, the chief of police, is forced to

114

re-examine the preconceptions and hasty judgments that have become habit. The result is a victory for justice, which in the outlook of at least one of its administrators is returned into alignment with the law.* Brownrigg's cynicism is jolted and he becomes again the idealistic humane 'servant of justice' he once was. Johnston's centre of interest in *Blind Man's Buff* was the individual caught up in the wheels of the law. In *Strange Occurrence* his attention is riveted exclusively on the machinery of justice and Brownrigg is the only character who changes at all in the course of the action, and then only in his professional life.

This final act of Johnston's Toller-free courtroom play is a *réchauffé* 'pot of message' so blatantly and rhetorically served up that instead of creating sharper critical awareness of the institutions we live by, it annoys an audience which has been caught up in the whodunit entertainment of the first two acts and then suddenly finds itself required to alter its expectations when the play moves into the embarrassing moralizing of the third act. Myles na Gopaleen (Brian O'Nolan), the famous satirist, was so struck by the banality of *Strange Occurrence* that he remarked on it in his column in the *Irish Times*: 'The theme is obviously concerned with crime, police, mystery, — regarded by me as the meanest form of literary pseudosity. . . . Mr. Johnston . . . gives us in his latest play moments which seem to embalm the thought of some other, quite unpractical fellow.' [9]

Strange Occurrence on Ireland's Eye is a considerable technical improvement over the clumsy farce and comedy bits of *Blind Man's Buff*. Yet the earlier play, for all its ineptitude, memorably communicates the dramatist's passionate involvement in his material. *Strange Occurrence* is a play that dies in the mind when the curtain falls.

---

*It is interesting to note that Johnston felt it was necessary 'to soften down the plot of the play' to make the real events credible. In the play, Kirwan is exonerated and released. In actuality, Kirwan was exonerated, but his death sentence was only commuted to life imprisonment, not rescinded. History can be more ironically tragic than fiction: Kirwan 'served the standard term for a life sentence' though his innocence was officially acknowledged. A thorough account of the Ireland's Eye case may be read in *Famous Irish Trials* by M. McDonnel Bodkin, K.C. (James Duffy: Dublin, 1928), pp. 106-128.

THE SCYTHE AND THE SUNSET

If his first play in sixteen years was a disappointment, the next (and last to date) was vintage Johnston. In his Easter 1916 drama *The Scythe and the Sunset* (Abbey Theatre, 1958) Johnston wrote an Irish history 'play that should re-establish him as our most clear-sighted commentator on the new Ireland and its beginnings.' [1] Most at ease among the passions and paradoxes of Irish life, Johnston was at the height of his powers as he returned to the landscape of his earliest and best-known plays — the Ireland of idealism and ineptitude where the drama of the birth of independence is played out by a handful of fervent self-styled patriots while the Irish populace for whom they zealously sacrifice themselves look on as an inimical and derisive audience. In *The Old Lady Says 'No!'* and *The Moon in the Yellow River* Johnston had portrayed the disjunctive aftermath of revolt. The action of both plays was roughly contemporary with their productions; they were designed to show Ireland to herself while she was in the violent process of searching for a national identity. In this sense they were activist plays, works of immediate relevance that endured because they captured without simplification or partisanship the complex post-revolutionary atmosphere of upheaval and perplexity. In contract, *The Scythe and the Sunset* is an analytic play, a retrospective fantasia composed from a forty-one year vantage point. Its subject is the seminal event in contemporary Ireland's struggle for liberty, the event which Seán O'Casey called 'the year One in Irish history and Irish life'.

Surprisingly, considering the almost legendary position Easter Week occupies in the Irish imagination, this spectacular insurrection has been the subject of only one play that has achieved any currency, Seán O'Casey's riot-provoking *The Plough and the Stars* (1926). Johnston was disturbed that the Irish theatre offered the world only a 'debunking' picture of 1916: 'I cannot accept the fact that, theatrically, Easter Week should remain indefinitely with only an anti-war comment, however fine.' [2] *The Scythe* is Johnston's attempt to balance the image. Johnston had no intention of trying to supersede O'Casey's play with a more accurate one. The two plays ought to be read in tandem, with the later play providing a view of the Rising in the light of subsequent historical development, from the overall world context of twentieth century political change. Johnston strives, in Grattan Freyer's phrase, to treat his material 'with full intelligence'. He tries to be as fair and impartial as a playwright can be who selects a particularly highly emotionally charged moment in his nation's destiny and uses that moment to illustrate his idea of historical process and of the inter-relation of chance and individual choice and responsibility in the making of history. In *The Scythe,* Johnston shuns the extremes which Conor Cruise O'Brien describes as an 'easy contempt for other people's nationalism' and an 'exaltation' of the men of '16, in favour of a 'comedy of argumentation and attitude'[3] that incorporates a variety of personalities, ideals, motives, actions and reactions. Johnston places the week in its international context which reveals it as more than an innocuous domestic squabble in the midst of worldwide conflagration. Johnston's remarkable achievement in *The Scythe* is his dual perception of the concrete and universal aspects of Easter Week. He presents both the detailed, moment-to-moment human motives—contradictory, illogical, exasperating—that under-lie history's headlines and an informed assessment of the Rising's place in a world-historical context.

The impulse to parody O'Casey that Johnston had controlled since *The Old Lady* is activated briefly in this play. Johnston's title (used twenty-five years earlier for a scene of *A Bride for the Unicorn*) is an 'obvious parody' of O'Casey's and the repetitive tenement dialect ('tantararums' and 'derogatory') that is a stock O'Casey device proves an irresistible quarry. But the parodic urge quickly consumes itself, for Johnston's purpose is deeper than lampoon. It is, as in most of his plays, to take up his characteristic stance of re-examiner. He re-opens the case of Easter, 1916, in order to take a fresh look at the 'official' versions, to sift fact from fantasy and to reconcile history and behaviour. He sets out in *The Scythe* to bring history into alignment with personal experience. Though Johnston was barely fifteen at the time, memories of his own involvement remain fresh and biting:

> I was a schoolboy at the time of the Rising, and for the greater part of three days my home was occupied and fortified by four male members of De Valera's battalion, while we of the family were held, supposedly as prisoners, but actually as hostages. . . . It all sounds more dramatic than it was. Our captors were soft-spoken and apologetic young men who did

the least damage they could. . . . On the third day, feeling I suppose that they had done enough for Ireland, they stripped off their accoutrements and disappeared. . . .

Consequently my recollections of the week are personal and undramatic. Of the rebels, I principally remember their charm, their civility, their doubts, and their fantastic misinformation about everything that was going on. Of the men in khaki there remains an impression of many cups of tea, of conversations about everything except the business in hand, and of a military incompetence of surprising proportions, even to my school-boy's eye.

. . . .

I have listened to many accounts of those last days, as described to me by men who had run the gauntlet of O'Connell Street under fire, and I remember very clearly the conversations of the rebels in my own home. But what I recollect most clearly of all is the aspect of Easter Week that is the most happily glossed over today — the intense hostility with which the whole affair was regarded by the Dublin public. At this distance it is hard to realize the widespread contempt in which the "Sinn Fein Volunteers" were generally held prior to the Rising. . . . It is probable that this contempt was more instrumental in driving the Volunteers into action at that time than any political or economic motives. "Face", not slogans, is one of the most powerful motivating forces . . . and these men had to prove that they were soldiers, or disband in the face of ridicule.[4]

In these passages Johnston implicitly outlines one of his primary concerns in The Scythe: to recapture the scene and action as he experienced it — another engagement in the determined John-stonian campaign to de-romanticize perpetuated melodramatic impressions. As one critic of The Scythe cleverly noted, Johnston 'undramatizes'[5] the Rising. This un-dramatization, however, is not undramatic. In The Scythe Johnston undertakes a new interpreta-tion of a 'sacred subject' which demands the full range of his intellectual and histrionic powers.

*   *   *

118

As O'Casey did with pub and slum, Johnston displaces the action of Easter Week from the urban battleground to a setting representing the antithesis of idealism. *The Scythe* takes place entirely in a sleazy restaurant which is comandeered by the rebels for a medical post. Into this café Johnston packs: three rebel leaders, two partially modelled on the contrasting personalities and goals of Pearse and Connolly; an ordinary patriotic Irish Volunteer; two contrasting British officers, one a native Irishman of shrewd political insight, the other a bumbling public school gift to the colonial forces; two women, one a Cumann na mBan extremist of the Maud Gonne or Countess Markiewicz variety, the other a dark Rosaleen, representative of the typical hostility of the average Dubliner toward Ireland's saviours; an oracular madman; and an urbane psychiatrist who serves as an epigrammatic commentator on the week's action. Johnston moves this cast through four crucial phases which span the week chronologically from the unexpected occupation of the G.P.O. to the rebel decision to surrender unconditionally. With these materials Johnston builds a tri-level pyramid of meaning: at the base an anti-melodramatic reconstruction of events; in the centre a few 'fanciful . . . dramatic inventions' which embody an ironic vision of historical processes; at the apex the persistent themes of his thought.

The opening scene typifies the fusion of action, attitude and shifting mood sustained throughout *The Scythe*. The interplay of sarcastic badinage, incompetent idealism and sudden violence recalls the atmosphere of *The Moon in the Yellow River*. As the Rising erupts, Johnston begins to expose the intricate chains of motive, choice, chance, error and luck — the minute threads which are haphazardly woven into the fabric of history. Accident is the rule, not the exception; the frequency of mishaps, the careful rendering of the farcical aspects of history, led one critic to call *The Scythe* 'the most hilarious of Johnston's comedies'.

As he had in *The Moon in the Yellow River*, Johnston couches within the hilarity and zaniness a lifelong commitment to psychological and political realism, to the dispelling of idealized myths and false images of heroism. Unlike Yeats's Pearse, Johnston's Tetley is not Cuchulain's protégé, a modern reincarnation of the heroic temper. Nor is he the pawn of an 'antiheroic' vision like O'Casey's offstage Pearse, eager to kill his people to win for himself a place in the pantheon of martyred patriots. Tetley is not actuated by grandiose vanity or altruistic heroism, though he is both vain and brave. Tetley is a 'humane and well-intentioned' man — neither saint nor hero — dedicated to an idea in which he has invested his prestige. Johnston insists that 'Men do not act from logical motives as often as they act under the promptings of the urge that . . . the Orientals call "face".' [6] Pared to this absolutely clear statement is the central tenet of Johnston's historical imagination: historical change springs from men protecting their images of themselves, whatever these images are called — face, prestige, pride, vanity, honour. Tetley explains: 'Now is the time to strike. . . . If we wait any longer . . . this generation will go down in history as being craven as the last. Personally, I'm not going to accept that.' And in Ireland there is always an Emer at hand to romanticize and heroicize what amounts to self-protection: 'In years to come, every decent man in Ireland will be wishing he could say, "I was in the Post Office in 1916".'

Most of the action in *The Scythe* can be traced to choices based on impulsive face-saving rather than on careful evaluation of fact or intelligent military guesswork. Individual irrationality (the victory of emotion over intelligence) and its effect on history is most compellingly presented in the incident of Palliser and the machine gun. Johnston painstakingly presents the British prisoner as a reasonable, expedient, politically acute professional soldier. For him there is no heroism, just competence or incompetence, British or Irish. One is either a soldier or an amateur who has no business playing at war. Palliser is so instinctively a professional that, irritated at their clumsiness, he can barely resist instructing the rebels in the operation of the gun when it is first captured, nearly betraying his own cause. He regains his self-control and in the second act emerges as the most farsighted political analyst in the Empire. He counters Clattering's argument for an artillery barrage:

> This mustn't be treated as a military operation. . . . A lot of fireworks will only make them look important. . . . Let's march them [the rebels] through the streets without their pants and ship them off in a cattleboat to their friends — the Huns. That'll put "paid" to the whole business. . . . I want to make *them* look damn silly. . . . It's the answer. I know this country.

History will corroborate Palliser's estimate that when 'the Crown makes martyrs' instead of pranksters out of the rebel leaders, it causes the 'intense hostility' of the Irish people to be transformed into a climate of sympathy and support that will sustain a guerilla insurgency.

His foresight and shrewdness, however, do not immunize Palliser against the spurs of pride. At the end of Act Two, when Emer contrasts Palliser and Tetley, and accuses Palliser of fearing death, he proves as susceptible as Mickser or Tetley to challenge to self-image. The Rising is about to end and leave Palliser without an opportunity to *show* Emer his courage. So, in a totally selfish burst of fury, he rigs the gun, which she fires to disrupt the negotiations and extend the fighting. Later, in Act Three, Tetley attributes Palliser's deed to a spirit of fair play: 'I believe you did it because you didn't want to see your countrymen climb down without putting up a good fight.' Palliser, who will die cursing the British failure to quell the Rising intelligently, is ashamed at having succumbed to what Endymion calls the Irishman's *'Gaes'* — a compulsive urge to behave irrationally. He counters Tetley: 'I did it for no such melodramatic reason. . . . Who wants to be thanked for letting himself be talked into playing the other fellow's game.' Even a politically sophisticated man will gaily forget consequences and throw common sense into the wind to guard his good name.

Efforts to win recognition or maintain self-esteem (even against one's better judgment) are not the sole factors in the forging of history. History is made not by clear-cut cause and effect, but by myriad, unpredictable combinations of self-interested choice, purblind political judgment and sheer fortuitousness, rarely joined by clearsighted evaluation. *All* the action of *The Scythe* is structured to illustrate the multiple causes of 'large events'. Take, for example, Tetley's imminent martyrdom at the play's close. In order for the rebellion to succeed in marshalling popular support, that is, as Shaw said of it, to 'work up a hare-brained Romantic adventure into a heroic episode in the struggle for Irish freedom', the leaders must be publicly and brutally executed. Tetley, contrary to the romantic myth of Pearse, doesn't 'want to be a martyr at all'. He only grasps the potential unifying power of self-sacrifice when Roisin is converted to the nationalist cause by O'Callaghan's death ('I've just seen a man die for his country — his country and mine'):

You saw how that shopgirl behaved over O'Callaghan. What will she feel — what will the nation feel — when fifteen or twenty of us have been treated to our "just deserts"?

He judges accurately for once:

> . . . this week can be turned from a disgrace into a triumph — all our mistakes and incompetence can be made of no importance whatever by giving ourselves up to some fool of a general.

Yet had Palliser's vanity not been taunted by Emer, had monomaniacal Emer not fired the gun at the moment a surrender was being negotiated, had the British not retaliated with heavy artillery and co-operatively sent Maxwell to settle the Irish question and immortalize the sixteen dead men, and, it ought to be added, had Michael Collins not been waiting in the wings to galvanize new sympathies into action, the rebellion would have failed, as all the rebels expected it would. The forces shaping history range from noble purpose and selfless love to self-love, from punitive sadism to ardent nationalism. By such multifarious threads is Johnston's loom of history fed.

To de-glamourize without debunking, Johnston treats most of the action of *The Scythe* as freewheeling farce. For instance, at one point a rebel will endanger the entire Rising rather than shoot a man in the back and imperil his immortal soul or his idea of his own gentlemanliness. Since Johnston's subject is not just history, but *Irish* history, bloodshed is inseparable from farce. However, beyond the minute concrete analysis of the farcical course of the Rising, Johnston always evokes a sense of Easter Week as part of a broader historical horizon. Ireland, without her knowing it, was playing a pioneering role in the British Empire's rendezvous with destiny. We are constantly aware that the play concerns 'not an Irish but a world phenomenon', that we are witnessing 'the opening phase in Dublin . . . [of] the passing of an imperial civilization'.[7] In O'Casey's bleak view, Easter Week was the nativity of a juggernaut of bloodletting. But Johnston sees 'more ways from Sackville Street than one'. His Endymion enters the scene for the final time in act three to lead his partner, an imaginary Britannia, in a stately and sorrowful dance of death:

Goodbye, my love.
Familiar things must now be put away.
Hard-riding squires
Drink the last stirrup cup of power.

. . . .

The April wind blows cold on royalty,
Swift, Grattan, Sheridan, Wellington and Wilde,
Levees on Cork Hill,
The tramp of crimson sentries in the colonnade.
No more of Suvla Bay or Spion Kop.
The bunting under which we spilled our colours on the globe
Shall hang in gaunt cathedrals
Where no one goes.

Actions attributable to face-saving motives, like Palliser's rigging
the machine gun, become pieces in a bigger pattern of what Palliser
himself calls the 'loosen[ing] of the foundations of a civilization'.
Ineptitude and stupidity emerge as unwitting moves in the end-
game of British colonialism. All the blunders made in the service
of face take on an aura of historical inevitability. Palliser recognizes
this and accepts it with chagrin at the play's close:

We always . . . play . . . the other fellow's game. We deserve
whatever's coming to us. . . . I know what's coming. . . . I see
it all as if it had happened already. Ireland's only the start.
We're going to go on winning every war, but piece by piece
we're going to give it all away.

The fact that the Rising had ramifications extending beyond the
immediate (and foiled) goals of the rebels was not its only source
of value and significance. In *The Scythe,* Easter Week is not
transformed into a consequential event only by virtue of historical
hindsight. Johnston has not de-romanticized legend in order to
make way for new legends. Johnston finds intrinsic value in the
Rising which is clearly visible once the obscuring myths are
uprooted. He gives the rebels their due:

. . . the affair, on the whole, was a humane and well-intentioned
piece of gallantry. And the more one sees of how these

123

uprisings have since been conducted elsewhere, the more reason everybody has to be pleased with Easter Week. In those days nobody had much experience of warfare, or of what would be likely to occur if the British Army were challenged in open rebellion for the first time in three or four generations . . . the Republicans must be credited considerable courage in taking the field at all; and in at least two engagements in the course of the week they showed military aptitude of the highest quality.[8]

When the initial 'game' of glass breaking, barricade and fusillade finally turns into 'warfare', the Rising takes on the power to arouse in its participants 'a deeper sense of the meaning of life'. Herein lies the 'virtue of violence'[9] — a theme Johnston fully elaborated in *A Fourth for Bridge*. Johnston rejects O'Casey's pacifism because war can offer an opportunity to achieve enduring self-value and a lasting recognition of communal bonds. Mickser Maginnis' transformation is a perfect example of the potential creativity of violence. At the opening of the play he is an impotent victim of internecine strife among the numerous nationalist factions. His frustration and rage (the most common emotional situation in modern Irish literature), usually expressed in querulous sarcasm, can also be channeled into military prowess. After his first engagement of the week, the unfortunate ambush of a party of elderly members of the Veteran Corps who were marching harmlessly without ammunition, Mickser is disgusted. Reality could only disappoint the great expectations Ireland's would-be heroes had always invested in the dream of an armed rising, 'that magic moment' when 'weakness and timidity and inexperience would fall'[10] from them and their impoverished lives would be redeemed. British military blatancy presents a chance for the rebels 'to turn wind into wonderment' as the brutal heavy artillery barrage arrests the growing disillusionment. Mickser's subsequent fighting in the Rising provides him with no less than his rescued manhood. War is an experience so overwhelming that the prosaic Mickser erupts into verse to describe it. It is not a question of heroism, for in this play there is no heroism and no cowardice, just professional soldiering and amateurish clumsiness. War doesn't make heroes, but it does help dreamers to make men of themselves. Mickser recounts his personal initiation into the 'exhilaration of conflict':

124

At first I was scared . . . scared that I was goin' to be
afeared. . . . But when it all got goin', I forgot. An' then when
I remembered, I sez to meself, "Begob, I forgot to be scared."
An' at that, God forgive me, I started to laugh, an' the most
unholy joy come over me, for I knew then I was a soljer, an'
nuttin' could ever take that from me.

Easter Week has made Mickser into the future Flying Column
guerrilla of the Black and Tan War — the professional soldier who
has adopted Palliser's credo that 'heroism is a second-rate ambition . . . another form of self-advertisement' and that what counts
in war is winning.

O'Casey's Easter Week in *The Plough and the Stars* is death-
dealing. He relentlessly denies the Rising any value. Johnston, in
contrast, refuses just as relentlessly to equate violence with evil.
Easter Week proceeded with no popular support and with maximum mismanagement on both sides, yet in the sphere of personal
experience it afforded many Irishmen their first sense of intense
aliveness and purposefulness. The Rising may have been tragic
in human terms or profound in international terms. But no matter
how it will be viewed as the perspectives of history change Johnston
claims it cannot merely be abhorred, for the very fighting of it
afforded the only self-respect many of its participants ever had.
The corollary of this, unfortunately, is: kill if it makes you feel
good. But Johnston ought not to be too easily accused of psychological fascism. The *fact* is that there is war and always has been.
Johnston does not believe that war can be abolished; it is a given
of the cycle of history. But does that mean man is evil? Yes —
partially, not absolutely. Johnston's quest, in his own experience
of war, was to determine whether anything in war redeems an
indictment of reality as absolutely evil. He finds his answer (in
Nine Rivers from Jordan) in the intensity of aliveness, of a feeling
of rebirth and attained manhood, in the front ranks. War and death
are accepted; Johnston says there is no alternative. And in them,
paradoxically, for such is Johnston's universe, life is enhanced.
There is an almost obligatory scene in Irish war dramas in which
a youth, cut down before he has any chance to live, dies in his
sweetheart's or mother's arms murmuring an act of contrition.
Johnston's characters had no chance to live *until* the Rising provided them with one. Mickser comes alive; O'Callaghan dies

smiling and Tetley might well like Pearse write *carpe diem* poems
on the eve of his execution. None, Johnston stresses, have anything
to regret.

*   *   *

In the series of impolite conversations between Palliser and
Tetley in acts two and three, Johnston gracefully dramatizes many
of the major themes of his mature thought. Ideological clash is
rooted in character and shares the urgency of the historical outbreak
of violence. Initially, contrasts abound in a confrontation of two
antipodal philosophies of life. Tetley is 'the man with the idea',
supremely confident that his life has a definable purpose. Naïve
idealist and military amateur, he expects the world to be as noble
as he. Palliser is 'the man of action' — the realist and professional
concerned only with effective and intelligent action, embarrassed
but not immobilized by his capture, registering all the ironies of
the rebellion's progress. In the early action of the Rising, Palliser
has the advantage of experience and his conviction that the rebels
will be quickly humiliated. He is scornful of Tetley's soldiering,
amused and distressed by the oversimplified certainties of Tetley's
idealism. Tetley, in turn, grows cavalier about the mysteries of
soldiering, on the basis of but a single day's experience, as Palliser
hastily points out in their second act encounter:

> Tetley.   Your profession is so terrifying, Captain — it's so
> simple. It requires no special qualities, except an
> indifference to one's personal fate that I find rather
> pleasant. . . . I've found since yesterday that soldier-
> ing gives one a great feeling of release — especially
> when you're bound to be beaten. . . . It doesn't
> require much courage to be shot at.
>
> Palliser.   So far, you've had damn little data on that.

Each approaches the other with rigid expectations based on his
own ethic. Palliser assumes that to save his skin Tetley would be
eager to repudiate his part in the Rising (Palliser: 'Why not? It's
a flop, isn't it?') and when Tetley answers: 'Whether it's a failure
or not, it has at least expressed the purpose of my life. You could
hardly expect me to repudiate that', Palliser is fascinated by the

126

combination of pomposity and determination. The exchange has passed from mutual scorn through a quarrel provoked by wounded vanity (despite irreconcilable differences they are both prey to a touchy pride) to the beginnings of curiosity and tentative mutual respect. It ends inconclusively:

Palliser. I'd rather like to see how much of a soldier you really are. There's more to it than this you know.

Tetley. *I'd* also like the chance of finding out.

Moments later Emer subtly manipulates Palliser into firing the gun and Tetley, with no effort on his part, has his chance.

By the third act, Tetley has proven himself a good pupil. The turn of events has made something of a realist of him. Now he perceives that surface failure need not preclude eventual success, since 'the man who loses is often the man who wins'. His execution will pave the way for a hopeless protest to inaugurate a successful guerrilla war: '. . . next time it will not be strictly in accordance with the rules.' In the previous act, when the rebellion was disintegrating, Tetley saw no reason for slaughtering Palliser and offered him his freedom, assuming that Palliser's realism made survival the first principle of his values. Palliser, calculating as realist, suspected Tetley's gesture had its price: 'Maybe you want me to pull a few strings for you? . . . I dare say I could get you off if we concocted a good story. . . . It's tit for tat. After all, isn't that why you're letting me go?' Ironically, the identical external situation recurs in this act, only now Tetley acts out of policy, not idealistic generosity — a measure of his growing realism. Palliser's testimony will be useful in assuring Tetley's conviction and punishment: 'You, Captain Palliser, will be subpoenaed, I'm afraid, as a star witness for the Crown.' Tetley still takes for granted Palliser's instinct for survival, but Palliser has alternatives:

Palliser. So that's the role you've picked for me.

Tetley. It's not my casting. It's Heaven that provides us with our roles in this fantastic pantomime.

Palliser. Well Heaven can't ballyrag me. I pick my own parts.

Palliser sees himself as free to make a responsible choice in full awareness of the consequences, the historical which are beyond his

127

control and the personal which he commands. Tetley is enthralled with success in the short run, but Palliser knows Tetley's martyrdom will be the origin of a chain of vengeance. Beyond *The Scythe* lie the Black and Tan War, partition and the Civil War. Palliser foresees the Ireland of *The Old Lady Says 'No!'* and *The Moon in the Yellow River*. He has already played his part in the creation of the cycle by rigging the gun. He cannot expiate past mistakes, nor does he want to. But he can refuse to make another mistake, to play a further part in instigating revenge. Rather than 'be a witness at [Tetley's] apotheosis', Palliser chooses to remain in the burning café. He elects to die in a private act that has no historical reverberations, for Tetley will be martyred anyway, but which contains its meaning wholly in itself. Yet Tetley has not become the realist and Palliser the idealist, for his choice rests too on its bit of vanity: 'It will show you and that bitch who's killing you for not marrying her [Emer] that there are other people who understand as much about death as you do.' Tetley, whose baptism under fire has converted him into a Johnston functionalist ('what's true is what works'), finds Palliser's decision, which he calls 'suicide', incomprehensible:

> You've got nothing to die for by stopping here. . . . Palliser, you're a fool. . . . If this is just a matter of showing off. I'm at least doing something the world will know about. But if you stop here until the building collapses, nobody will know about it except me.

On this matter there is an unbridgeable gap in their ethical views. Knowing Tetley will not understand, Palliser replies: 'I shall know about it myself'. Palliser will die to break the stranglehold of functional values which Tetley, who has lost his political innocence in the Rising, now asserts with history on his side. Tetley's death will *succeed*.

In this superbly dramatic climax, in which two men elect to die, each choosing out of fidelity to his philosophy of life and his self-image, Johnston incorporates an ironic vision of the conflict of realist and idealist in a specific historical context. Tetley, though he has ceased to be the 'innocent blessed with arms in [his] hands for the first time', as O'Casey described the men of '16,[11] remains dedicated to fulfilling the purpose of his life, which will depend upon forces outside of himself for its implementation and meaning.

He rejects Palliser's last-minute offer of collusion to get him off: 'Don't think you can bully me out of my destiny.' In contrast, Palliser will die in an act that 'must be its own reward, . . . relying on no illusions or hopes for the future to give it importance'.[12]

Tetley sees only glory in his martyrdom, but Palliser sees it as the birth of a cycle of vengeance, whatever its value in the killing of colonialism. Palliser refuses to sanction Tetley's illusions, and towards the close of their dialogue he attempts to force Tetley into an awareness of the cycle that is being set in motion and of the futility of his idealism. Palliser, as he begins to respect Tetley's determination and courage though he deplores its success, tries to make Tetley realize that he (Palliser) has a great deal to die for — his freedom:

> . . . don't be too proud. . . . It won't be the first time people like you have loosened the foundations of a civilization. . . . You'll have it in chains again, as you had before. But not me. . . . You don't give a damn about liberty. All you care about is a cause. And causes always let you down. Your admirers will find that out before they're finished.

Tetley is shaken by this uncomfortable frankness and insight, but neither will deviate from his choice. They part as official enemies but closer as men, and, though each desperately wants the other's side to lose, they respect each other's total truth to himself.

Though *The Scythe and the Sunset* deals with history antecedent to *The Moon in the Yellow River*, it is in many thematic ways a sequel to *The Moon*. Lanigan was trapped in the cycle of revenge. Dobelle was fortunate; he could repudiate the cycle and survive. Palliser, an actor in history, does not enjoy the privilege of the private citizen; history decrees that, to shun the perpetuation of evil, Palliser must die. His death, like Dobelle's renunciation, has no perceivable effect on history, for a single man refusing to play the villain's role is not remarkable; a substitute can always be found. Yet the option to write one's own role when one can is an act of faith and freedom. Palliser's death is a declaration of independence proclaimed without any illusion of effectiveness, without hope of future immortality.

Dobelle, Dotheright, Anice Hollingshead, John Foss, the Acolyte of *Nine Rivers from Jordan,* Palliser — all exemplify Johnston's faith in man's capacity for redemption. Johnston's is a gospel of 'self-help' and personal responsibility unrelated to a worldly gospel of efficiency — the man who loses is often the man who wins. Beginning with *The Moon in the Yellow River,* Johnston has been developing a recurring central pattern of idea and feeling; *The Scythe* is the latest piece of the figure emerging from Johnston's carpet. The duty of the Johnston hero is to strive continually for clarity of vision and constant vigilance so that he will not himself contribute to the continuance of evil. He comes to recognize his duty only after the fall, for he must live in the world and know good and evil, unadorned. Focusing on the problem of evil Johnston's plays are theological dramas; but they are simultaneously dramas of self-discovery. The Johnston hero is disenchanted but undismayed by his knowledge of the ways of the Functionalist world. Palliser reads and quotes Blake, a profound inspirer of Johnston's ideas. All his major characters sing in turn songs of innocence and experience (except Palliser whom we meet fully-formed), each has faced facts absolutely and recognized and accepted the contradictions that shape reality, the interpenetration of good and evil. They reject oversimplification, having learned that:

> People can't really be divided into heroes and villains, cowardice is as universal as fortitude and just as natural, the common-sense of today is the collaboration of tomorrow, and that while our real acts of courage and virtue pass unnoticed, the medals and honours that we wear on our breasts are usually just matters of luck. We know these things from experience and if we have any sense we don't resent them any more than we resent the rain.[13]

Ceasing to combat reality in the world or within oneself is the path to maturity and self-realization, and the spring-board from alienation or self-involvement to pity, love and community:

> It is not outside, but within himself, that Man finds the self without which he cannot be complete. It is only in the willing acceptance of those apparent contradictions in human behaviour . . . that life and character can be realized to the full and Man can achieve his real greatness.[14]

130

Palliser and company exemplify 'the redemption which all men have in their nature';[15] they are embodiments of a 'conception of man . . . the purpose of whose life is itself, not a future life in some other world — whose immortality is not of another world, but of this one.'[16]

The tremendous optimism implicit in Palliser's death represents a notable change in Johnston's outlook, always realistic but not always 'cheerfully realistic'. Hilton Edwards said to me recently that Johnston's ideas haven't altered since the earlier plays. This judgment should be qualified; Johnston's philosophy has been essentially constant since World War II. The original version of *The Moon* (1931) ended bleakly in a welter of 'death and darkness'. The revised version (1959 — but incorporating changes made over twenty-eight years) ended interrogatively, Dobelle's pessimism shifting to doubt as he wonders if there is any cure for vengefulness. *The Scythe* is rounded off with a resounding declarative, a curtain line Johnston borrowed from his own sermons in praise of life:

Winter gives back the roses to the frost-filled earth.

The splendid affirmation with which *The Scythe* ends (and *Nine Rivers to Jordan*) is an eloquent disproof of the serious charge Edwards made in 1946 that:

Denis' genius is two-sided in everything. It is not by any means that he is sitting on a fence but it makes for a lack of commitment, a feeling of caution in the theatrical sense of his plays and in the actors' and directors' approaches, however much it is a central aspect of his philosophy.[17]

It is a pity that Johnston even today is misunderstood by the best director he has had. All of his work is a testament to Johnston's commitment — to historical and moral realism (though his dramaturgy may urge this realism through radical stylization) and to a joyous philosophy of hope and unsentimental pity earned by fearless confrontation of fact. Denis Johnston has superbly heeded Synge's famous plea: 'On the stage one must have reality, and one must have joy.'

Chronology

1901   William Denis Johnston born 18 June.

1908–   Attends St. Andrew's College, Dublin.
1915

1915–   Attends Merchiston Castle School, Edinburgh.
1917

1923   Receives baccalaureate in law from Cambridge (Christ College).

1924   Pugsley Scholar, Harvard Law School.

1925   Called to English, Irish and Northern Irish Bars.
        February: Plays the role of King Gustavus Adolphus in Jacinto Benavente's *The School of Princesses,* a Drama League production.
        April: Appears in *Fanny's First Play* at the Abbey.
        December: Plays Cusins in Mme. Hackett's Irish premiere of Shaw's *Major Barbara.*

1926   July: Plays *Ulysses* in Euripides' *Cyclops* at Drama League.

1927   May: Plays Roberto in *The Constant Nymph* at Abbey.
        November: Plays Guido Venanzi in Pirandello's *The Game as He Played It,* Drama League.
        Produces Kaiser's *From Morn to Midnight* for The New Players.

1928   March: Plays Nojd in Strindberg's *The Father,* Drama League.
        Uses the pseudonym E. W. Tocher which remains his theatrical name until 1936.
        Plays the Student in Evreinov's *The Chief Thing,* a New Players production.
        May: Produces O'Neill's *The Fountain* for Drama League.
        November: Produces *King Lear* for the Abbey.
        December: Marries the Abbey actress Shelah Richards.

1929   March: Produces Toller's *Hoppla* for Drama League.
        July: Johnston's first play, *The Old Lady Says 'No!'* opens at the Gate Theatre.

1931	April: Johnston's ballet, 'The Indiscreet Goat', opens as part of the Gate's *Dublin Revue.* *The Moon in the Yellow River* opens at Abbey on 27th.
1933	May: *A Bride for the Unicorn* opens at Gate. December: Plays Terrence in Mary Manning's *Youth's the Season* . . . at Gate.
1934	January: *Storm Song* opens at Gate. April: Produces Mary Manning's *Happy Family* at Gate. Autumn: Produces the first wholly Irish film, the Gate's production of Frank O'Connor's *Guests of the Nation.*
1936	April: Plays in Lord Longford's *Armlet of Jade* and O'Neill's *Ah, Wilderness!* at Westminster Theatre, London. December: *Blind Man's Buff,* adapted from Toller's *The Blind Goddess,* opens at Abbey.
1936– 1938	Script writer, BBC radio, Belfast.
1938	September: Script writer, BBC television.
1939	April: *The Golden Cuckoo* opens at Gate.
1940	March: *The Dreaming Dust* opens at Gaiety Theatre, Dublin, a Gate production.
1941– 1942	Drama critic, *The Bell,* Dublin.
1942– 1945	BBC war correspondent.
1945	Divorces Shelah Richards. Marries (March 25) the Gate actress Betty Chancellor.
1946	Awarded OBE.
1947	Drama Critic, Radio Eireann, Dublin. Writes only one-act play, *A Fourth for Bridge.*
1947– 1949	Writes for NBC Theatre Guild of the Air in New York.
1949– 1950	Visiting Professor, Amherst College, Massachusetts.
1950– 1967	Professor of Drama at Mount Holyoke and Smith Colleges, Massachusetts.

1953   *Nine Rivers from Jordan,* an autobiography of the war years.

1956   May: *Tain Bo Cuailgne,* a pageant presented in Dublin. August: *Strange Occurrence on Ireland's Eye* opens at Abbey.

1957   Produces Mary Manning's dramatization of *Finnegans Wake* at Yale University.

1958   March: *The Scythe and the Sunset* opens at Poet's Theatre, Cambridge, Massachusetts, and at Abbey in May.

1959   *In Search of Swift,* a biography.
April: Hugo Weisgall's opera, *Six Characters in Search of an Author,* libretto by Johnston, opens at City Center, New York.

1960   *Siege at Killyfaddy,* television play.

1967   Settles in Channel Islands.

1969   Hugo Weisgall's opera, *Nine Rivers from Jordan,* libretto by Johnston, opens at City Center.

Brief Stage Histories

The original casts of the plays are readily available in the published editions. Only important productions are listed.

The Old Lady Says 'No!'
Première at Peacock Theatre, 3 July, 1929.
American première, May 1935, at Amherst College.
English première, June 1935.
Gate company production in New York, February, 1948.
BBC TV production, 1964.

The Moon in the Yellow River
Première at Abbey Theatre, 27 April, 1931.
New York Theatre Guild production, New York, 29 February, 1932, starring Claude Rains.
Produced at 1934 Malvern Festival under the auspices of George Bernard Shaw.
In 1934/35 *Moon* runs almost 200 performances in London.
1937 — plays in Melbourne and Warsaw.
1938 — first TV version.
1954 — radio version.
Revived in New York, 1961.
Produced by Arena Stage, Washington, D.C., 1962.

The Moon is the most produced of Johnston's plays; as he once remarked: 'Very few little theatres have resisted its production.'

A Bride for the Unicorn
Première, Gate Theatre, 9 May, 1933.
Produced by the Harvard Dramatic Club, 1934.
London première, July, 1936.
Radio version, 1938.

Storm Song
Première, Gate Theatre, 30 January, 1934.
English première, 6 July, 1936.
After a Melbourne production in 1938, Johnston withdrew the play from the boards.

135

Blind Man's Buff
Première, Abbey Theatre, 28 December, 1936.
London première, September, 1938; revived 1953.

The Golden Cuckoo
Première, Gate Theatre, 25 April, 1939.
London première, January, 1940.
American première, Provincetown Playhouse, August, 1950.
Revived by Cyril Cusack in Dublin, June, 1956.

The Dreaming Dust
Première, Gate Theatre, March 25, 1940.
English première, Bristol Old Vic, 1946.
American première, Provincetown Playhouse, July, 1954.
Revived at the Dublin Theatre Festival, September, 1959.

Strange Occurrence on Ireland's Eye
Première, Abbey Theatre, 20 August, 1956, ran seven weeks.
Radio version, 1956.

The Scythe and the Sunset
Première, Poets' Theatre, Cambridge, Massachusetts, 14 March, 1958.
Irish première, Abbey Theatre, 19 May, 1958. TV version, 1965.

Notes

Introduction

1 Denis Johnston, 'Plays of the Quarter', *The Bell,* vol. 2, no. 1 (April, 1941), 90.
2 Lennox Robinson, Letter to James Stephens, quoted in Michael J. O'Neill, *Lennox Robinson* (New York: Twayne, 1964), p. 113.
3 O'Neill, p. 114.
4 *Ibid.,* 113-114.
5 *Joseph Holloway's Irish Theatre,* Robert Hogan and Michael J. O'Neill (eds.), vol. I, (California: Proscenium Press, 1968), p. 43.
6 *Lady Gregory's Journals 1916-1930,* Lennox Robinson (ed.), (New York: Macmillan, 1947), pp. 112-118.
7 *The Gate Theatre — Dublin,* Bulmer Hobson (ed.), (Dublin, 1934), p. 21.
8 Thomas Hogan, 'Denis Johnston', *Envoy,* III (August, 1950), p. 34.
9 Una Ellis-Fermor, *The Irish Dramatic Movement* (London: Methuen, 1964), p. 188.
10 *Ibid.,* pp. 7-8.
12 Quoted in Grattan Freyer, 'The Irish Contribution', *The Modern Age* ('The Pelican Guide to English Literature', vol. 7 [Boris Ford, ed.]; Middlesex: Penguin Books, 1961), p. 200.
13 Interview with Denis Johnston, 29 March, 1965.
14 Denis Johnston, 'The Present State of Irish Letters', 1947 (Manuscript in the files of Denis Johnston).
15 Lady Augusta Gregory, *Our Irish Theatre* (New York: Capricorn Books, 1965), p. 91.

The Old Lady Says 'No!'

1 Denis Johnston, 'Seán O'Casey: An Appreciation', *Living Age,* vol. 329, no. 4267 (April, 1926), 162.
2 *The Irish Statesman,* 20 July, 1929, p. 390.
3 P. S. O'Hegarty, *Motley,* vol. II, no. 2 (February, 1933), 12.
4 Micheal MacLiammoir, *All for Hecuba* (Dublin: Progress House, 1961), pp. 78-80.
5 Interview with Hilton Edwards, 4 March, 1966.
6 Denis Johnston, 'Opus One', *The Old Lady Says 'No!' and Other Plays* (Boston: Atlantic, Little, Brown, 1960), p. 18.
7 Denis Johnston, 'Let There Be Light', *The Old Lady Says 'No!' and Other Plays,* p. 3.
8 Denis Johnston, 'Waiting with Beckett', *Irish Writing,* (Spring, 1956), p. 25.
9 Unpublished 'Introduction' to the play in the possession of the author.
10 Johnston, 'Opus One', p. 17.
11 Denis Johnston, *Shadowdance* (1926), unpublished manuscript in the possession of the author.
12 Micheal MacLiammoir, 'Problem Plays', *The Irish Theatre,* ed. Lennox Robinson (London: Macmillan, 1939), p. 219.

13 Unpublished 'Introduction' to the play.
14 Hilton Edwards, 'Denis Johnston', *The Bell*, vol. 13, no. 1 (October, 1946), p. 11.
15 Mac Liammoir, 'Problem Plays', p. 219.
16 Lennox Robinson, *The Dreamers* (London: Maunsel, 1915).
17 Johnston, 'Opus One', p. 15.
18 C .Curran, *The Irish Statesman*, 13 July, 1929, p. 375.
19 Arland Ussher, *The Face and Mind of Ireland* (New York: Devin-Adair, 1950), p. 91.
20 C. Curran, 'Foreword', *Two Plays by Denis Johnston* (London: Cape, 1932), p. 10.
21 Curtis Canfield, 'A Note on the Nature of Expressionism and Denis Johnston's Plays', *Changing Plays of Ireland* (New York: Macmillan, 1936), p. 33.
22 Patrick O'Donovan, 'The Right Way to Wear the Green', *The New Republic*, 153 (11 September, 1965), p. 21.
23 Timothy Patrick Coogan, *Ireland Since the Rising* (London: Pall Mall, 1966), p. xi.
24 *The New York Times*, 8 January, 1965, pp. 1, 10.
25 Denis Johnston, *The Golden Cuckoo and Other Plays* (London: Cape, 1954), p. 8.

The Moon in the Yellow River

1 Edwards, 'Denis Johnston', p. 11.
2 Interview with Denis Johnston.
3 *Ibid.*
4 *Irish Times*, 8 April, 1931, p. 8.
5 Denis Johnston, 'Let There Be Light', p. 3.
6 Denis Johnston, 'Period Piece', *The Old Lady Says 'No!' and Other Plays*, p. 3.
7 Denis Gwynn, *The Irish Free State* (London: Macmillan, 1928), pp. 319-336.
8 Olivia H. G. Hughes, 'The Shannon Scheme As A Woman Sees It', *The Irish Statesman*, 23 October, 1926, p. 153.
9 *The Ottawa Citizen*, 4 December, 1954.
10 Denis Johnston, Programme Note to Amherst College Masquers production of *The Moon in the Yellow River*, May, 1950.
11 Ellis-Fermor, p. 203.
12 Johnston, 'Let There Be Light', p. 3.
13 Stuart Gilbert (ed.), *Letters of James Joyce* (New York: Viking, 1957), p. 118.
14 Johnston, 'Preface', *The Old Lady Says 'No!' and Other Plays*, p. 9.
15 *Times Literary Supplement*, no. 3059 (14 October, 1960), 656.
16 Freyer, 'The Irish Contribution', p. 204.
17 Robert Corrigan, 'The Plays of Chekhov', *The Context and Craft of Drama* (Robert Corrigan and James L. Rosenberg, eds.) (San Francisco: Chandler, 1964), p. 150.
18 Curtis Canfield, *The New York Times*, 25 November, 1934, p. 17.

19 Stark Young, *The New Republic,* 70 (16 March, 1932), 127.
20 W. B. Yeats, *The Collected Poems* (New York: Macmillan, 1957), pp. 201-202.
21 See, for example, R. M. Fox, 'The Cult of the Machine', *The Irish Statesman* (5 November, 1927), 199.
22 Patrick Pearse, *Political Writings and Speeches* (London: Maunsel and Roberts, 1922), p. 336.
23 W. B. Yeats, Letter to Katharine Tynan, quoted in John Unterecker, *A Reader's Guide to William Butler Yeats* (New York: Noonday, 1959), p. 42.
24 Edwin Burr Pettet, 'The Enduring Anti-Heroic', *The Massachusetts Review* (Summer, 1961), 788.
25 Canfield, 'A Note . . . ', pp. 35-36.

A Bride for the Unicorn
1 This happy phrase was coined by Robert Brustein.
2 Ellis-Fermor, p. 202.
3 John Jordan, 'The Irish Theatre — Retrospect and Premonition', *Contemporary Theatre,* Stratford-upon-Avon Studies 4 (London: Arnold, 1962), p. 172.
4 Denis Johnston, *The Golden Cuckoo* . . . , p. 5.
5 Edwards, 'Denis Johnston', p. 13.
6 William York Tindall, *Forces in Modern British Literature,* (New York: Vintage, 1956), p. 73.
7 Hilton Edwards 'Production', *The Gate Theatre — Dublin,* p. 36.
8 Hans Meyerhoff, *Time in Literature* (Berkeley: University of California, 1955), p. 3.
9 J. B. Priestley, *Midnight on the Desert* (New York: Harper, 1937), p. 244.
10 David Hughes, *J. B. Priestley* (London: Rupert Hart-Davis, 1958), p. 142.
11 Denis Johnston, *Nine Rivers from Jordan* (Boston: Little, Brown, 1955), p. 336.
12 *The Evening Standard* (London), 2 July, 1936.
13 J. W. Dunne, *The Serial Universe* (London: Faber, 1934), p. 36.
14 Gareth Lloyd Evans, *J. B. Priestley — The Dramatist* (London: Heinemann, 1964), pp. 57-58.
15 Anna Balakian, *Surrealism: The Road to the Absolute* (New York: Noonday, 1959), pp. 93-161.
16 Johnston, *Nine Rivers,* p. 443.
17 *Ibid.,* p. 445.
18 Evans, p. 58.
19 Denis Johnston, 'For a Preface to *The Unicorn*', unpublished manuscript in the possession of the author.
20 William York Tindall, *The Literary Symbol* (Bloomington: Indiana, 1955), p. 164.
21 *Ibid.*
22 Michael Grant, *Myths of the Greeks and Romans* (New York: World, 1962), p. 300.

23 Johnston, 'For a Preface to *The Unicorn*'.
24 Denis Johnston, 'Lecture on Yeats', unpublished manuscript in the possession of the author.
25 Georges Sorel, 'Reflections on Violence', *Myth and Myth-making,* ed. H. A. Murray (New York: Braziller, 1960), p. 360.
26 Edwards, 'Denis Johnston', p. 12.
27 Interview with Denis Johnston.
28 Una Ellis-Fermor, *The Frontiers of Drama* (London: Methuen, 1967), p. 12.
29 Denis Johnston, 'Letter to a Young Dramatist', *The Listener,* vol. LVI (August 30, 1956), 305.

The Sense of an Ending

1 G. S. Fraser, *The Modern Writer and His World* (London: Verschoyle, 1952), p. 164.
2 Johnston, 'Preface', *The Old Lady Says 'No!' and Other Plays,* p. 9.
3 Tindall, *Forces . . .* , p. 73.
4 MacLiammoir, *All for Hecuba,* p. 164.
5 Edwards, 'Denis Johnston', pp. 12-14.
6 Thomas Kinsella, *Nightwalker and Other Poems* (Dublin: Dolmen, 1968).

Storm Song and Blind Man's Buff

1 Johnston, *The Golden Cuckoo . . .* , p. 6.
2 Hogan, 'Denis Johnston', p. 41.
3 Edwards, 'Denis Johnston', p. 15.
4 Interview with Denis Johnston.

The Golden Cuckoo

1 Johnston, *The Golden Cuckoo . . .* , pp. 10-11.
2 *Ibid.,* pp. 8-9.
3 Denis Johnston, 'The Irish Theatrical Renaissance as a Cultural and Social Force'; manuscript in the possession of the author.
4 Johnston, *The Golden Cuckoo . . .* , p. 11.
5 *Ibid.,* p. 12.
6 *Ibid.*
7 Albert Camus, *The Rebel* (New York: Vintage, 1956), p. 14.

The Dreaming Dust

1 Denis Johnston, 'The Trouble with Swift', *The Nation,* vol. 196, no. 4 (26 January, 1963), 73.
2 L. A. G. Strong, *The Sacred River* (New York: Pellegrini and Cudahy, 1951), p. 77.
3 James S. Atherton, *The Books at the Wake* (New York: Viking, 1960), p. 118.
4 Denis Johnston, *The Dublin Historical Record,* vol. III, no. 4 (June-August, 1941), 81.

5   *Ibid.*, 82.
6   *Irish Times,* 26 March, 1940, p. 4.
7   J. J. Hayes, *Christian Science Monitor,* 27 April, 1940, p. 11.
8   Johnston, *The Golden Cuckoo* . . . , p. 16.
9   Johnston, *The Dublin Historical Record,* p. 82.
10 Johnston, 'Period Piece', pp. 3-4.
11 William Butler Yeats, *Explorations* (London: Macmillan, 1962), p. 362.
12 Johnston, *The Golden Cuckoo* . . . , p. 15.
13 *The New Yorker,* vol. 36, no. 159 (26 March, 1960), 159.
14 Frank Kermode, *The Spectator* (6 November, 1959), 639.
15 Oliver St. John Gogarty, 'The Enigma of Swift', *Intimations* (New York: Abelard, 1950), p. 81.
16 Edwards, 'Denis Johnston', p. 16.
17 Johnston, 'Period Piece', p. 5.
18 Denis Johnston, Sermon delivered at Mount Holyoke College, 22 November, 1954; manuscript in the possession of the author.
19 Johnston, *Nine Rivers,* p. 442.

A Fourth for Bridge and *Strange Occurrence on Ireland's Eye*
1   Johnston, *The Golden Cuckoo* . . . , p. 17.
2   *Ibid.*
3   *Ibid.,* pp. 17-18.
4   Johnston, *Nine Rivers,* pp. 134-135.
5   Kaspar Spinner, *Die Alte Dame Sagt: Nein!* (Bern: A. Francke, 1961), p. 191.
6   Denis Johnston, 'Arma Virumque', *The Old Lady Says 'No!' and Other Plays,* p. 3.
7   Johnston, *Nine Rivers,* p. 136.
8   Pettet, 'The Enduring Anti-Heroic', p. 787.
9   *Irish Times,* 27 August, 1956, p. 6.

The Scythe and the Sunset
1   *Irish Times,* 4 July, 1951, p. 5.
2   Denis Johnston, 'Up the Rebels', *The Old Lady Says 'No!' and Other Plays,* p. 4.
3   *Times Literary Supplement* (14 October, 1960), 656.
4   Johnston, 'Up the Rebels', pp. 5, 9-10.
5   Pettet, 'The Enduring Anti-Heroic', p. 786.
6   Johnston, 'Up the Rebels', pp. 10-11.
7   *Ibid.,* p. 11.
8   *Ibid.,* p. 10.
9   Johnston, *Nine Rivers,* p. 137.
10 James Joyce, *A Portrait of the Artist as a Young Man* (New York: Modern Library, 1944), p. 71.
11 Quoted in Roger McHugh, (ed.), *Dublin 1916* (London: Arlington, 1966), p. 251.
12 Carole Corcoran, Course Paper for Harvard Univerity, unpublished manuscript in the possession of Denis Johnston.

13 Denis Johnston, 'We'll Keep You in Mind', BBC Radio Talk, 13 June, 1948; manuscript in the possession of the author.
14 Johnston, 'Lecture on Yeats'.
15 Corcoran.
16 Johnston, 'Lecture on Yeats'.
17 Interview with Hilton Edwards.

A Selected Bibliography

1. BY DENIS JOHNSTON

PLAYS

Blind Man's Buff. London: Jonathan Cape, 1938.
The Golden Cuckoo and Other Plays. London: Cape, 1954.
The Old Lady Says 'No!' and Other Plays. Boston: Atlantic, Little, Brown, 1960.
Storm Song and A Bride for the Unicorn. London: Cape, 1935.
Two Plays. London: Cape, 1932.
Toller, Ernst and Denis Johnston. *Blind Man's Buff.* New York: Random House, 1939.

BOOKS

In Search of Swift. Dublin: Allen Figgis, 1959.
John Millington Synge. New York: Columbia, 1965.
Nine Rivers from Jordan. Boston: Little, Brown, 1955.

ARTICLES ON THEATRE AND IRISH LITERATURE

'The College Theatre — Why?', *Theatre Arts,* XLIV (August, 1960), 12-15.
'Drama — The Dublin Theatre', *The Bell,* III (February, 1942), 357-360.
'Joxer in Totnes', *Irish Writing,* 13 (December, 1950), 50-53.
'Letter to a Young Dramatist', *The Listener,* LVI (30 August, 1956), 305-308.
'The Mysterious Origin of Dean Swift', *The Dublin Historical Record,* III, 4 (June-August, 1941), 81-97.
'Plays of the Quarter', *The Bell,* volume 2, number 1, (April, 1941), 89-92.
'Seán O'Casey: An Appreciation', *Living Age,* volume 329, number 4267 (April, 1926), 161-163.
'Seán O'Casey, A Biography and an Appraisal', *Modern Drama,* (December, 1961), 324-328.
'That's Show Business', *Theatre Arts,* XLIV (February, 1960), 82-83.
'Towards a Dynamic Theatre', *The Gownsman* (8 June, 1935), 22.
'The Trouble with Swift', *The Nation,* volume 196, number 4 (26 January, 1963), 73.
'Waiting with Beckett', *Irish Writing,* 34 (Spring, 1956), 23-28.
'What Has Happened to the Irish', *Theatre Arts,* XLIII (July, 1959), 11-12.

2. ABOUT DENIS JOHNSTON

Browne, E. Martin, 'Introduction', *Three Irish Plays* (Middlesex: Penguin, 1959), 7-8.
Canfield, Curtis, 'A Note on the Nature of Expressionism and Denis Johnston's Plays', *Changing Plays of Ireland* (New York: MacMillan, 1936), 25-36.

Edwards, Hilton, 'Denis Johnston', *The Bell*, volume 13, number 1 (October, 1946), 7-18.

Hogan, Robert, 'The Adult Theatre of Denis Johnston', *After the Irish Renaissance* (Minneapolis: Minnesota, 1967), 133-146.

Hogan, Thomas, 'Denis Johnston', *Envoy*, III (August, 1950), 33-46.

McCarthy, Mary, 'Little Theatre', *Sights and Spectacles* (New York: Farrar, Strauss, 1956), 136-140.

Mercier, Vivian, 'The Plays of Johnston', *The Nation*, 194 (13 May, 1961), 416-417.

Pettet, Edwin Burr, 'The Enduring Anti-Heroic', *The Massachusetts Review* (Summer, 1961), 785-788.

Phillipson, Wulstan, 'Denis Johnston', *The Month*, 25 (June, 1961), 365-368.

Spinner, Kaspar, *Die Alte Dame Sagt: Nein!, Drei Irische Dramatiker: Lennox Robinson, Seán O'Casey, Denis Johnston* (Bern: A. Francke, 1961).

3. SUGGESTIONS FOR FURTHER READING

Coogan, Timothy Patrick, *Ireland Since the Rising* (London: Pall Mall, 1966).

Did You Know That the Gate . . . ? (Dublin, 1940).

Dobrée, Bonamy, 'Seán O'Casey and the Irish Drama', *Seán O'Casey*, ed. Ronald Ayling (London: Macmillan, 1969), 92-105.

Edwards, Hilton, *The Mantle of Harlequin* (Dublin: Progress House, 1958).

Ellis-Fermor, Una, *The Irish Dramatic Movement* (London: Methuen, 1964).

Freyer, Grattan, 'The Irish Contribution', *The Modern Age* (Penguin, 1961), 196-208.

Hobson, Bulmer (ed.), *The Gate Theatre* — Dublin (Dublin, 1934).

Jordan, John, 'The Irish Theatre — Retrospect and Premonition', *Contemporary Theatre* (London: Arnold, 1962), 165-184.

MacLiammoir, Micheal, *All for Hecuba* (Dublin: Progress House, 1961).

MacLiammoir, Micheal, *Theatre in Ireland* (Dublin, 1964).

Robinson, Lennox (ed.), *The Irish Theatre* (London: Macmillan, 1939).